MEL BAY'S COMPLETE
JAZZ GUITARMETHOD

MW00989211

By Mike Christiansen

CD CONTENTS*

1. Introduction/Tuning
2. Swing Rhythm
3. Barre Chords (root on the sixth string)
4. Barre Chords (root on the fifth string)
5. Barre Chords (combined categories)
6. Dead-String Chords (root on the sixth string)
7. Dead-String Chords (root on the fifth string)
8. Dead-String Chords (combined categories)
9. Barre Chords Combined with Dead String Chords
10. Bass-String Chords (root on the sixth string)
11. Bass-String Chords (root on the fifth string)
12. Bass-String Chords (combined categories)
13. Comping
14. Comping
15. Comping
16. Chord Inversions
17. Chord Inversions
18. Altered Seventh Chords
19. Altered Seventh Chords
20. Major Scale Solo
21. Major Scale Rhythm Track
22. Major Scale Rhythm Track
23. Major Scale Solo
24. The m7b5 Chord
25. Solo Over The m7b5 Chord
26. Natural Minor Scale Solo
27. Harmonic Minor Scale Solo
28. Melodic Minor Scale Solo
29. Jazz Minor Scale Solo
30. Minor And Major Scales Solo
31. Major And Minor Scales Solo
32. Chord Embellishment
33. Chord Substitution
34. Chord Embellishment And Substitution

35. Blues Progression (basic)
36. Blues Progression (variation)
37. Blues Progression (variation)
38. Blues Progression (variation)
39. Minor Blues Progression
40. Minor Pentatonic Scale Solo
41. Minor Pentatonic Scale Solo
42. Minor Pentatonic Scale Solo
43. Blues Scale Solo
44. Blues Scale Solo
45. Sequencing Solo (major scale)
46. Sequencing Solo (harmonic minor scale)
47. Sequencing Solo (minor pentatonic scale)
48. Sequencing Solo (major pentatonic scale)
49. Diminished Chords
50. Diminished Scale Solo
51. Augmented Chords
52. Whole Tone Scale Solo
53. Latin Rhythms
54. Latin Rhythms
55. Latin Rhythms
56. Dorian Mode Solo
57. Dorian Mode Solo
58. Dorian Mode Solo
59. Mixolydian Mode Solo
60. Solo Combining Modes
61. Solo Combining Modes
62. ii-V-I Rhythm Track
63. ii-V-I Rhythm Track
64. Solo Over ii-V-I
65. Solo Over ii-V-I
66. Lydian Mode Solo
67. Solo Combining Modes
68. Aeolian Mode Solo

69. Phrygian Mode Solo
70. Locrian Mode Solo
71. Super Locrian Mode Solo
72. Arpeggios
73. Arpeggios
74. Arpeggio Rhythm Track
75. Arpeggio Solo
76. Solo With Arpeggios
77. Solo With Arpeggios
78. Solo With Arpeggio Sequences
79. Solo With Targeting
80. Solo With Guide Tones
81. Phrasing
82. Building A Solo
83. Building A Solo
84. Soloing Using 7ths And 9ths
85. Secondary Arpeggios
86. Parker Cycle
87. Coltrane Cycle
88. Improvising Around A Melody
89. Improvising Around A Melody
90. Improvising Around A Melody
91. Improvising Around A Melody
92. Improvising Around A Melody
93. Quartal Harmony Blues (m7sus chords)
94. Quartal Harmony Blues (6/9 chords)
95. Chord Substitution Using Quartal Harmony (m7sus chords)
96. Chord Substitution Using Quartal Harmony (6/9 chords)
97. Solo Using Fourths
98. Solo Using Fourths
99. Solo With Geometrical Shapes

***This book is available as a book only or as a book/compact disc configuration.**

If you have purchased the book only, a recording (95384CD), and a video (95384VX) of the music in this book are now available. The publisher strongly recommends the use of these resources along with the text to insure accuracy of interpretation and ease in learning.

Visit us on the Web at www.melbay.com — E-mail us at email@melbay.com

Introduction

This book will present the various elements of jazz guitar and show how to combine those elements. Whether you are interested in playing swing, fusion, Latin or bebop, this method will be of great value in helping to focus your studies and understanding of the concepts involved in playing jazz guitar. The contents include sections on playing rhythm and single note soloing (improvisation). In each section, there are many examples and exercises. It's important that you not only practice the exercises and solos in this book, but that you apply the skills you will learn from playing the examples to playing jazz standards. As with learning any style of music on the guitar, learning to play jazz guitar may seem a bit overwhelming at first, but if you take each element of the style, break it down, and then combine the elements. With patience, you'll get it. To get the right "feel' for jazz, it's important you surround yourself with the music of guitarists who play jazz. However, don't limit your listening to guitarists only. Many great jazz guitarists say they have learned jazz by imitating horn players, pianists, and vocalists. As you listen to the music of guitarists like Joe Pass, Johnny Smith, Jim Hall, Wes Montgomery, Mike Stern, John Schofield, Pat Matheney, and others, analyze what they are doing. Listen for the different ingredients in their playing. At the same time, don't be too analytical. Before I took a geology class, I used to drive up the canyon and think how beautiful it was. Suddenly, after taking the class, I found myself analyzing the canyon and being concerned with how the different areas were formed. It took a while to get back to seeing the overall picture and appreciating the beauty of the whole. In your listening and playing, don't forget to hear the beauty of the whole picture and enjoy the music. Learn all the concepts contained in this book so well that using them comes naturally to you. Because you will be learning how to improvise, the possible ways of combining the ingredients (scales, modes, arpeggios, etc.) are limitless.

Due to copyright restrictions, this book does not contain jazz standards. But, the examples and exercises are written in such a way they can be applied to jazz standards or other jazz compositions. It is hoped (and expected) the student will get a jazz fake book and apply the concepts contained in this book. Enjoy!

This book is dedicated to Professor Larry G. Smith
with thanks for his friendship, tutoring, encouragement,
and contagious enthusiasm for jazz.

Contents

Diagrams

The chords and scales in this book are drawn on diagrams like the one shown below. These diagrams are pictures of the guitar neck. The vertical lines represent frets with the first fret at the top. The horizontal lines represent the strings with the first string on the right. The numbers on the lines show where to place left hand fingers. With the chords, a circle above the string indicates to play that string open. An "X" above the string indicates the string is not to be played. A black diamond shows where the root of the scale, or chord, is found.

A solid bar across several strings indicates one finger (usually the first finger) presses (bars) across more than one string.

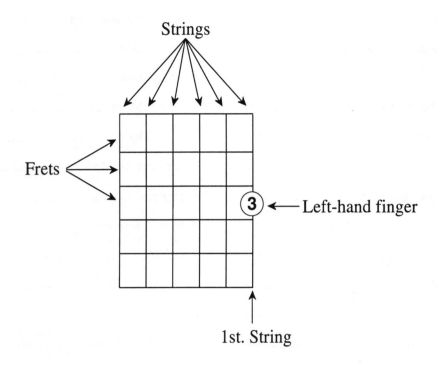

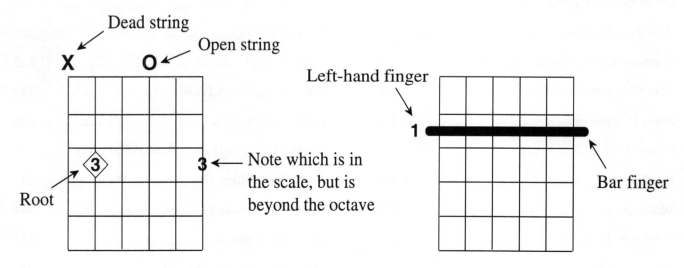

Chord Symbols And Abbreviations

The names of chords (symbols) in this book will be written in several different ways. The chart below will help you know the symbols used for the different chord names. One the right is written the type of chord. On the left are the various symbols used in writing the chord names. The notes contained in all of the chords will be presented in later sections of this book.

Major	major chords can be written with only the alphabet name (i.e. D, G, E. etc.). Major chords also be sharp or flat (i.e. B♭, E♭, F♯, etc.). Major chords can also be written as Maj. or with a capital M next to the letter name of the chord.
Minor	m, -
Augmented	aug., +
Diminished	Dim., o
Half Diminished	Ø
Suspended	sus, sus4
Sixth	6
Minor Sixth	m6, -6
Seventh	7
Major Seventh	maj7, M7, 7̶
Minor Seventh	m7, -7
Minor Major Seventh	m+7, m7
Seventh Suspended	7sus
Augmented Seventh	+7, 7+
Ninth	9
Major Ninth	maj9, M9, 9̶
Minor Ninth	m9, -9
Add Nine	add9, /9
Major Six Nine	6/9
Eleventh	11
Thirteenth	13

In altered chords, flat intervals can be written with a flat sign (♭) or a dash (-) before the name of the interval. For example, D seven flat nine would be written D7-9, or D7♭9. Sharp intervals in a chord can be written with a sharp sign (♯) or a plus sign (+) before the name of the interval. For example, E seven sharp nine would be written E7♯9, or E7+9. C seven, sharp five, flat nine would be written: C7♯5♭9, or C7+5-9.

Time Values

The following time values apply if the bottom number in the time signature is a 4. If the bottom number in the time signature is an 8 rather than a 4, all of the time values are doubled.

	NAME	TIME VALUE

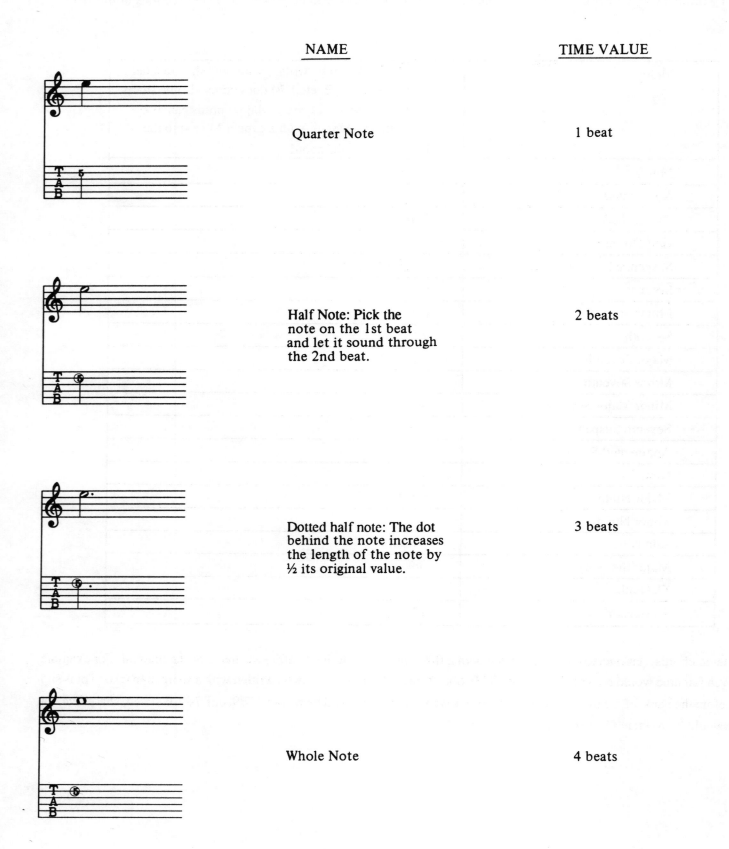

NAME	TIME VALUE
Quarter Note	1 beat
Half Note: Pick the note on the 1st beat and let it sound through the 2nd beat.	2 beats
Dotted half note: The dot behind the note increases the length of the note by ½ its original value.	3 beats
Whole Note	4 beats

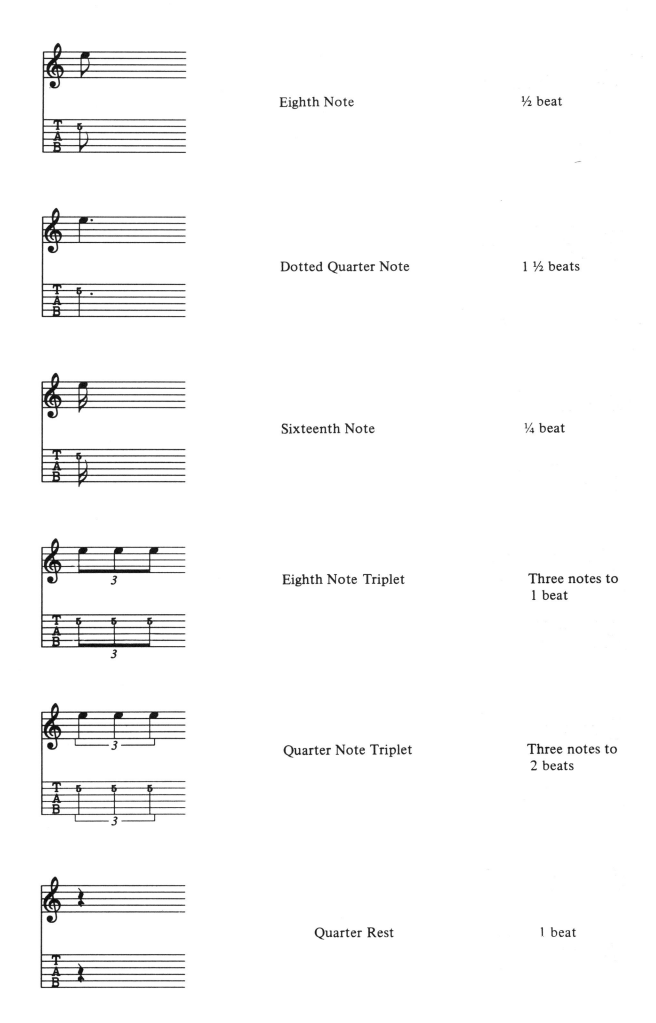

Eighth Note   ½ beat

Dotted Quarter Note   1 ½ beats

Sixteenth Note   ¼ beat

Eighth Note Triplet   Three notes to 1 beat

Quarter Note Triplet   Three notes to 2 beats

Quarter Rest   1 beat

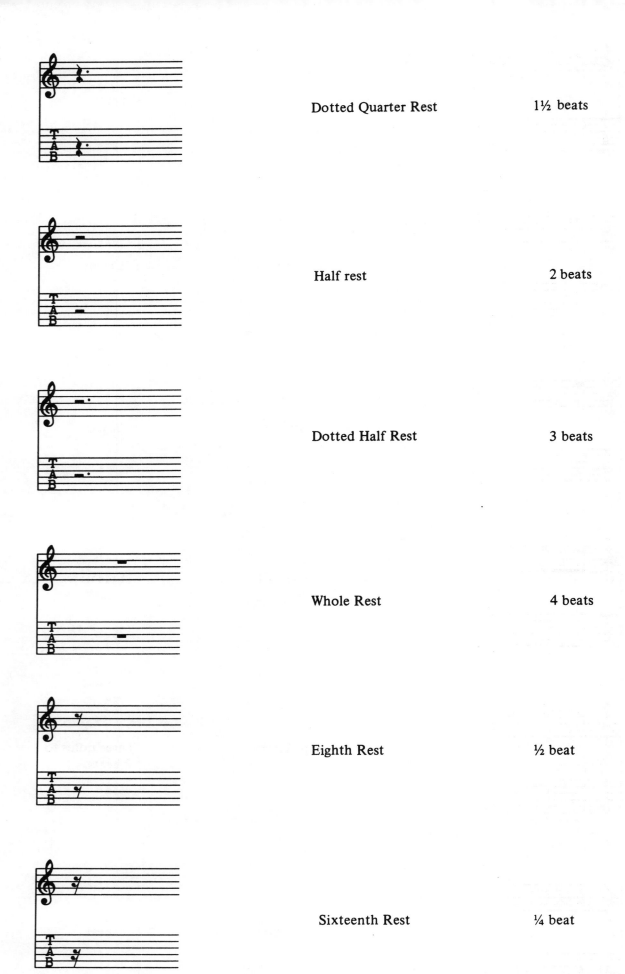

Dotted Quarter Rest   1½ beats

Half rest   2 beats

Dotted Half Rest   3 beats

Whole Rest   4 beats

Eighth Rest   ½ beat

Sixteenth Rest   ¼ beat

Shown in the measures below are how many of each kind of note it would take to complete one measure in 4/4 time. The measures have been stacked so that you can see the relationship of the notes to one another. For example, two half notes equal one whole note. The dotted lines show the separation of the beats in the measure.

Written in the measures below are the different kinds of notes it would take to complete one measure in 6/8 time. Remember, in 6/8 the eighth note gets one beat. Again, the measures have been stacked so you can see the relationship of the notes to each other.

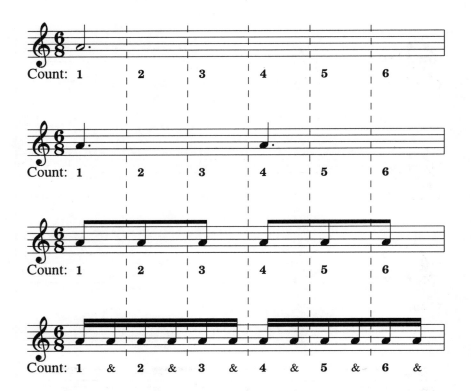

Syncopation

Syncopation means placing the accent on a beat (or a part of the beat) which is normally weak. Syncopation is often done by playing a note on the up beat (second half of the beat, or the *and*) and letting that note ring through the first half of the next beat. Syncopated rhythms are commonly written as a quarter note, or quarter notes, between two eighth notes. Sometimes the second eighth note is replaced by a dot after the quarter note. The following illustrations show how syncopated rhythms are written and how they are counted. Some of the songs, exercises, and solos in this book contain these rhythms. It's important that you understand how they are counted. Hold any note and practice tapping your foot on the beat while you play and count aloud the rhythms written below.

Swing Rhythm

Normally when two eighth notes are connected together (♫), the beat is divided into two equal parts. When playing jazz it's more common to use *swing rhythm*. This means the first eighth note is longer than the second, so the beat is divided into a long–short pattern. With swing rhythm, two eighth notes connected together are interpreted and played as though they were a one-beat triplet with the middle note tied (♫ = ♪♪♪).

If you have a hard time getting the swing feel, try thinking of the rhythm used in the "Battle Hymn of the Republic." This song is usually sung with swing rhythm. All of the single-string scales, solos, and exercises in this book should be played with swing rhythm unless the piece is Latin music. **Do not use swing rhythm when playing Latin styles (Bossa Nova, Samba, etc.).** Latin music is played with even eighth notes.

Swing rhythm is commonly used when playing the blues and is often referred to as "shuffle rhythm."

To get the swing feel, practice playing a single note over and over as in the example written below. First, play the eighth notes even and then swing them.

The examples in this book which have been recorded on the accompanying CD have a CD icon and number above them. The number corresponds with the number on the CD where the recording of the example is located.

This means the piece is to be played using swing rhythm.

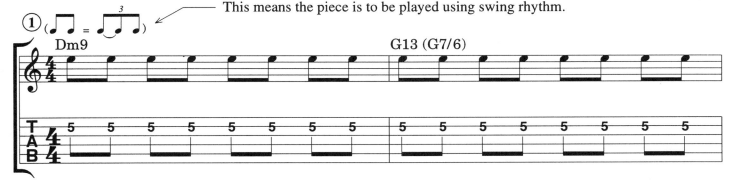

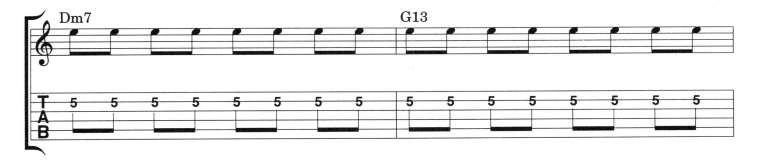

Next, practice a scale as eighth notes using swing rhythm.

The rhythm will swing even more if you accent the off-beats. The example below shows where the accents would occur.

Another technique used to make the music swing and have a better jazz feel is to accent the notes which precede and follow rests. The example below shows where these accents would be placed.

Unless you are playing a Latin style, use swing rhythm when playing the solos and exercises in this book and on your own improvised solos.

Strumming Notation

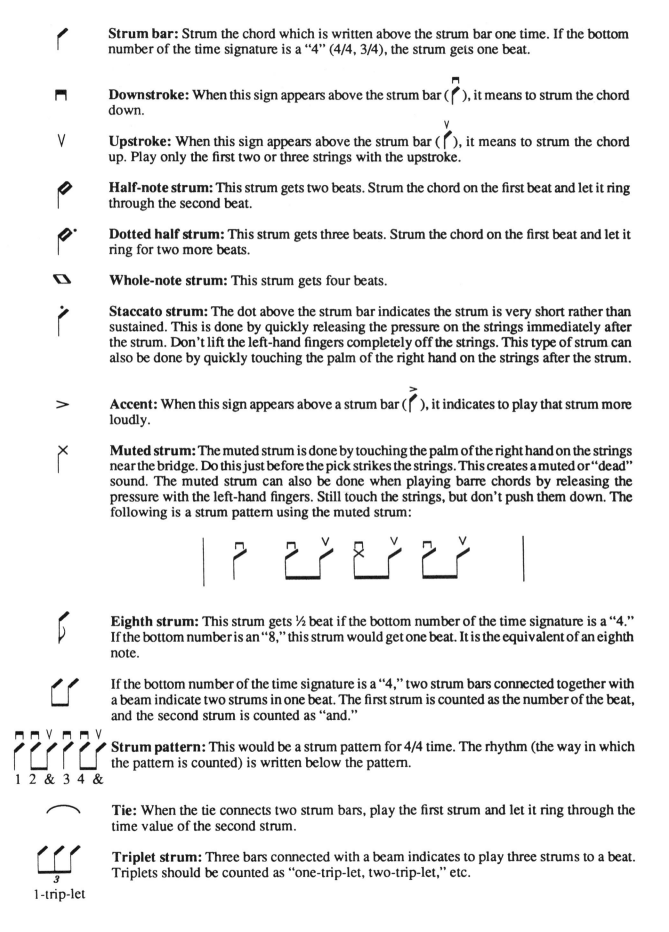

Strum bar: Strum the chord which is written above the strum bar one time. If the bottom number of the time signature is a "4" (4/4, 3/4), the strum gets one beat.

Downstroke: When this sign appears above the strum bar ( ), it means to strum the chord down.

Upstroke: When this sign appears above the strum bar ( ), it means to strum the chord up. Play only the first two or three strings with the upstroke.

Half-note strum: This strum gets two beats. Strum the chord on the first beat and let it ring through the second beat.

Dotted half strum: This strum gets three beats. Strum the chord on the first beat and let it ring for two more beats.

Whole-note strum: This strum gets four beats.

Staccato strum: The dot above the strum bar indicates the strum is very short rather than sustained. This is done by quickly releasing the pressure on the strings immediately after the strum. Don't lift the left-hand fingers completely off the strings. This type of strum can also be done by quickly touching the palm of the right hand on the strings after the strum.

Accent: When this sign appears above a strum bar ( ), it indicates to play that strum more loudly.

Muted strum: The muted strum is done by touching the palm of the right hand on the strings near the bridge. Do this just before the pick strikes the strings. This creates a muted or "dead" sound. The muted strum can also be done when playing barre chords by releasing the pressure with the left-hand fingers. Still touch the strings, but don't push them down. The following is a strum pattern using the muted strum:

Eighth strum: This strum gets ½ beat if the bottom number of the time signature is a "4." If the bottom number is an "8," this strum would get one beat. It is the equivalent of an eighth note.

If the bottom number of the time signature is a "4," two strum bars connected together with a beam indicate two strums in one beat. The first strum is counted as the number of the beat, and the second strum is counted as "and."

Strum pattern: This would be a strum pattern for 4/4 time. The rhythm (the way in which the pattern is counted) is written below the pattern.

1 2 & 3 4 &

Tie: When the tie connects two strum bars, play the first strum and let it ring through the time value of the second strum.

Triplet strum: Three bars connected with a beam indicates to play three strums to a beat. Triplets should be counted as "one-trip-let, two-trip-let," etc.

3

1-trip-let

Sixteenth strum: This strum gets ¼ beat if the bottom number of the time signature is a 4. If the bottom number of the time signature is an 8, this strum gets ½ beat.

1 e & a

Four strum bars connected with two beams indicate four strums to one beat. The strums should be counted "one-ee-and-a." It is the equivalent of four sixteenth notes.

Written below are various combinations of eighth and sixteenth notes. Notice the suggested strum directions and how the rhythms are counted. Hold any chord and practice these patterns:

⊓ ⊓ V   ⊓ V ⊓   ⊓ V V   ⊓ V   ⊓ V

1-& a   1 e &-   1 e - a   1--a   1 e--

Quarter rest: Rest for one beat if the bottom number of the time signature is a "4." If the bottom number is an "8," rest for two beats.

Eighth rest: Rest for ½ beat if the bottom number of the time signature is a "4," and rest for one beat if the bottom number is an "8."

Two-beat rest.

Four-beat rest.

Barre Chords

As with many other guitar styles, a knowledge of rhythm guitar playing is important not only if you are the rhythm guitarist, but a solid knowledge of chords is also invaluable to the soloist. This section of the book will present hundreds of chord form possibilities in such a manner that they should be fairly easy to pick up and understand. The first group of chords we'll be working with are *barre chords*. It is assumed that you are already familiar with the basic first position, or open chords.

Barre chords get their name from the fact that a finger (usually the first finger) bars or lies across all of the strings. There are two basic categories of barre chords. In the first category, the root of the chord (note which has the same letter name as the chord) is on the sixth string. When the bar finger is placed in a particular fret, the name of the note on the sixth string in that fret will be the letter name of the chord. The chart below shows the location of the note names (roots) on the sixth string. Below the chart are the barre chord patterns for the various types of chords. To find a particular chord, place the bar finger in the fret number which corresponds to the letter name of the chord. Then, hold the correct chord form for that type of chord. For example, Am7 would be played in the fifth fret like this:

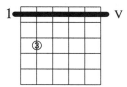

To sharp a barre chord, move the pattern up one fret. To flat a barre chord, move the pattern down one fret. For example, B♭7 would be played like this:

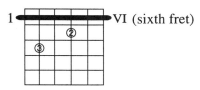

First Category
(Sixth String Root)

Fret ⟶	0	1	3	5	7	8	10	12
Root Name ⟶	E	F	G	A	B	C	D	E

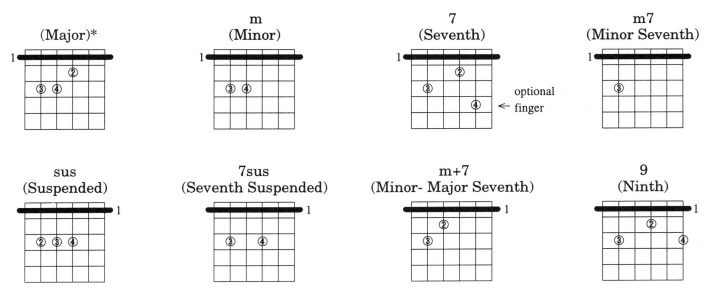

*Major chords are those in which the name of the chord is only a letter name (i.e. G, C, D, etc.). Major chords may also be sharp or flat.

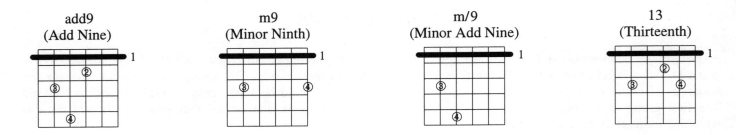

The following exercises use only barre chords from the first category. If you already know barre chords, you should still practice these exercises. They will introduce you to some common jazz chord progressions. Play each chord in the following set of exercises as a barre chord. If the exercise is in 4/4, strum down four times in each measure. If the exercise is in 3/4, strum down three times in each measure. Though it may seem oversimplified, one of the most popular strum patterns for jazz in 4/4 is to strum down four times in a measure. It will sound stylistically correct if you accent beats two and four (♩ ♩ ♩ ♩). In jazz it's also common to make each strum short by lifting the fingers up after each strum so the strings stop vibrating. This is sometimes called a staccato strum. Don't lift the fingers completely off the strings, and be careful not to make the strum too short and choppy. If the piece is in 3/4, strum down three times in a measure and place the accent on the first beat. For 3/4 you could also use this strum pattern in each measure: ♩ ♩ ♩ . In 3/4, you can also alternate the strum pattern and down three times every other measure: ♩ ♩ ♩ ♩ ♩ ♩ . These accompaniment patterns for 4/4 and 3/4 can be used to play most of the chord exercises in this book.

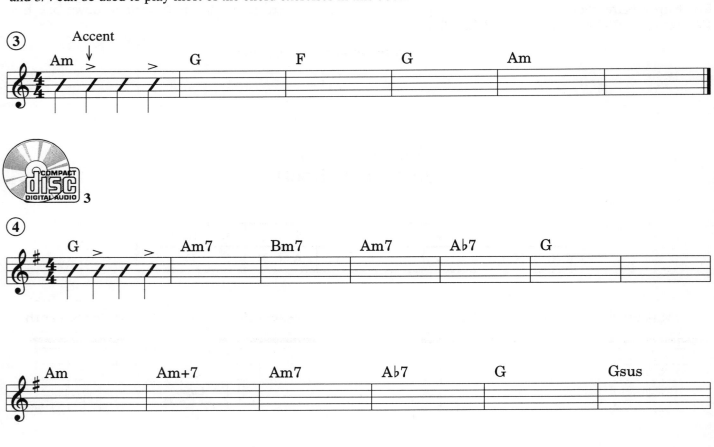

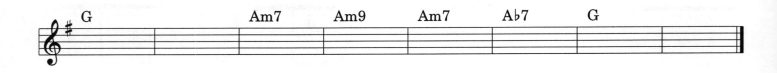

16

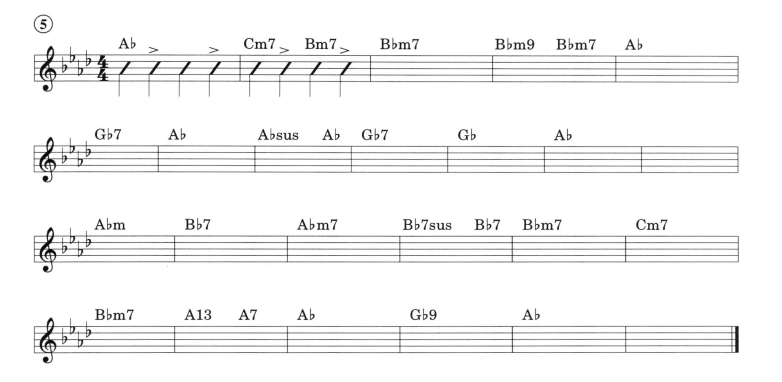

Second Category
(Fifth String Root)

With the second category of barre chords, the root is on the fifth string. Although the bar finger may go across all six strings, these chords may sound better if only five strings are strummed. This will make the root the lowest note heard. The chart below shows the location of the root names on the fifth string. Shown on the diagrams below the chart are the fingerings for each type of a chord. The same procedure is used to locate the chords as was used for the first category of barre chords. For example, a C♯m7 chord would be played like this:

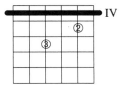

Remember, to flat a barre chord move the pattern down one fret, and to sharp a barre chord move it up one fret.

Fret →	0	2	3	5	7	8	10	12
Root Name →	A	B	C	D	E	F	G	A

Notice there are two different fingerings for some of the chord types (i.e. major and maj7). Use the pattern which is most convenient and/or sounds the best.

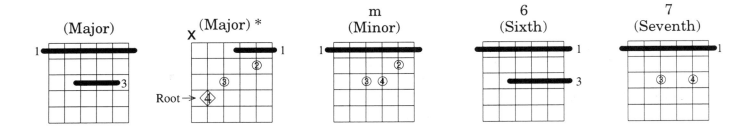

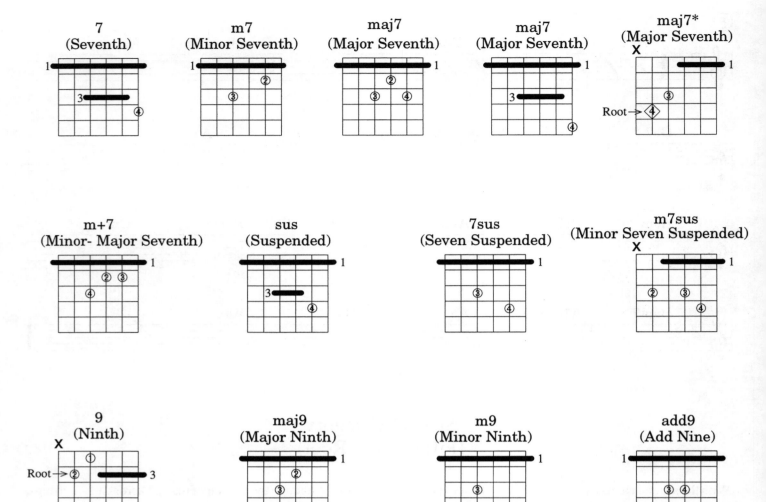

Practice the following progressions using only barre chords from the second category. Play every chord as a barre chord. Use what ever strum patterns you would like.

* These barre chords also have their roots on the fifth string. Though not as popular as the other major and maj7 fifth string root chords from this category, in some situations they are the best choice of patterns to use.

Knowing two categories of barre chords will make it possible to make chord changes more convenient and provides for good voice leading. This means that the notes from one chord lead smoothly to the notes in the next chord. Whether a chord is play from the first or second category will depend upon where the previous chord was played. For example, a chord change like Gm7 to C7 can be done be staying in the third fret and using Gm7 from the first category and C7 from the second category.

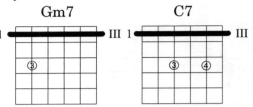

Practice the following progressions using barre chord form both categories. Try to keep the chords close to each other. The R/6 and R/5 above the chord names indicate whether the chord has the root on the sixth string (first category) or the fifth string (second category).

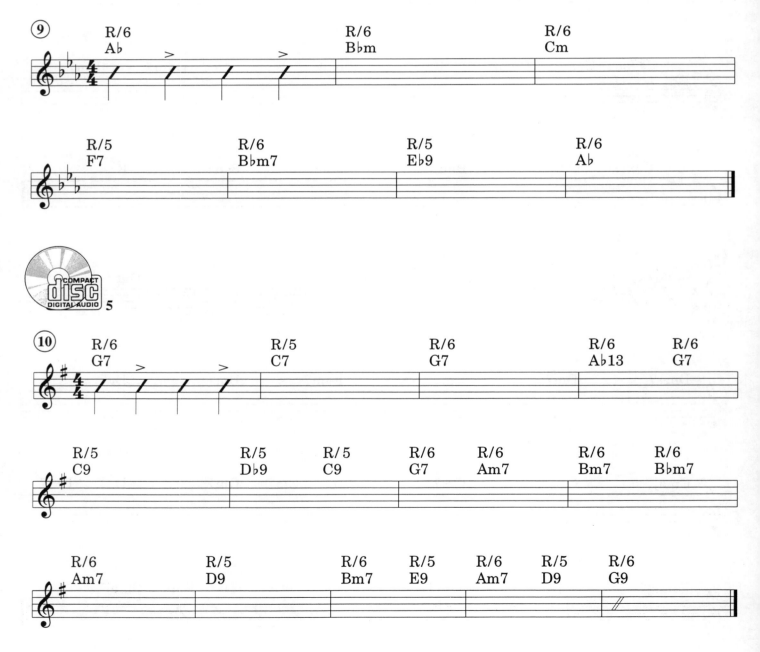

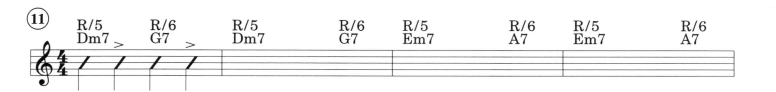

Dead-String Chords

A *dead-string chord* is one in which one or more of the strings is touched with a left-hand finger and dampened intentionally so that when the chord is strummed, those strings are not heard. These chord forms are commonly used in playing jazz guitar. Like barre chords, there are two categories: those with roots on the sixth string and those with roots on the fifth string. With some of the patterns, the root is not played. An example of this would be in the pattern for a ninth chord from the second category. If the root is not played, a circle will be drawn on the diagram showing the location of where the root would be. Even though you don't finger the root, you still have to know where it is located in order to position the pattern in the correct fret. To find the location of the roots, refer to the barre chord charts.

There are other dead string chords which are not included in these categories (i.e. altered chords). They will be presented in other sections of this book.

First Category
(Sixth String Root)

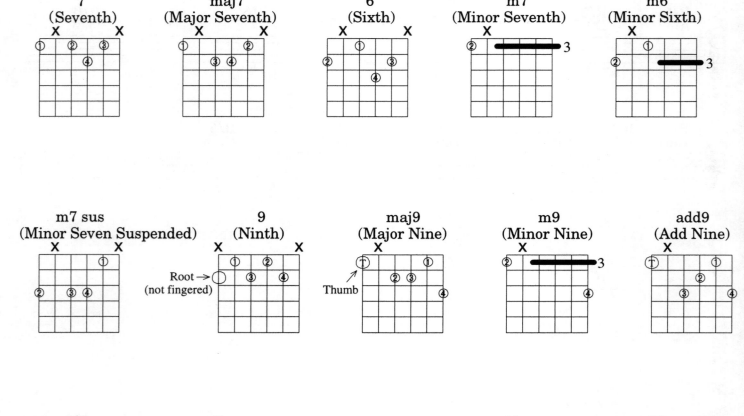

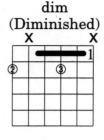
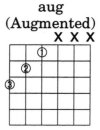
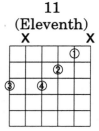
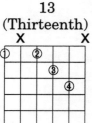

Practice the following progressions which contain dead-string chords from the first category. Strum four times down in each measure with accents on beats two and four.

Second Category
(Fifth String Root)

(Major)

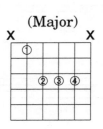

m
(Minor)

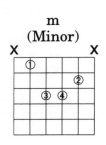

7
(Seventh)

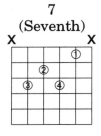

7sus
(Seventh Suspended)

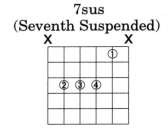

maj7
(Major Seventh)

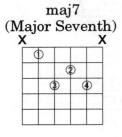

m7
(Minor Seventh)

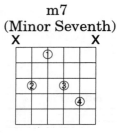

m7
(Minor Seventh)

m7
(Minor Seventh)

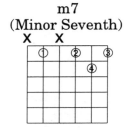

m7sus
(Minor Seventh Suspended)

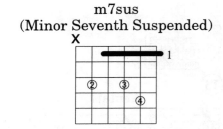

6
(Sixth)

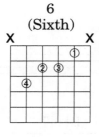

6
(Sixth)

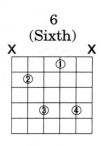

m6
(Minor Sixth)

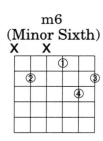

9
(Ninth)

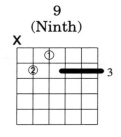

maj9
(Major Ninth)

m9
(Minor Ninth)

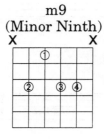

6/9
(Major Six Nine)

dim
(Diminished)

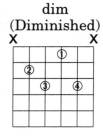

11
(Eleventh)

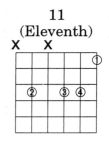

aug
(Augmented)

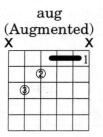

The following progressions should be practiced using dead-string chords from the second category.

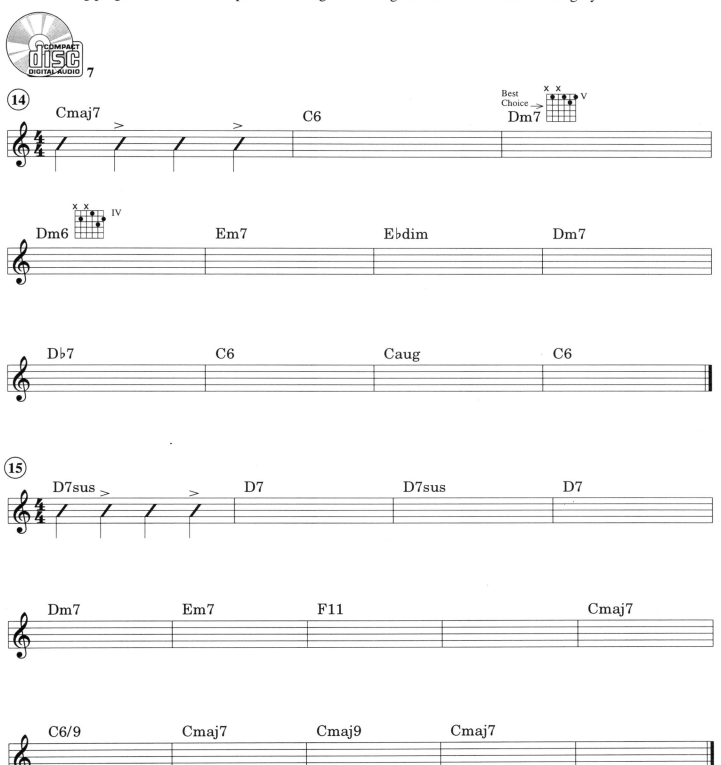

As with barre chords, knowing both categories will keep the chord changes closer together. Practice the following progressions using dead-string chords. The R/6 and the R/5 above the chord names indicate whether the root of the chord is on the sixth or the fifth string. This will help you determine whether to use a dead-string chord from the first or the second category.

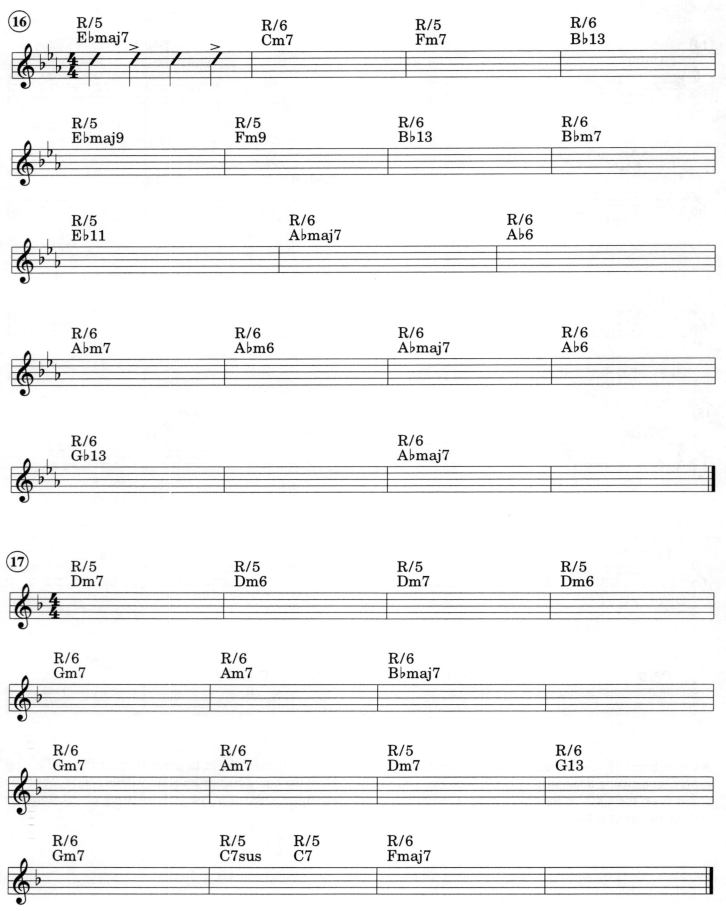

8

Dead-string chords are often used in conjunction with barre chords. Practice playing the following progressions which combine barre chords withe dead-string chords. The rule is: if it can't be played as a barre chord, it's probably a dead-string chord. To help to determine whether to use a dead-string chord or a barre chord, in the first two examples below, a "B" (representing "barre") or "D" (dead-string) has been written above the chord name. In the third example, you decide which to use.

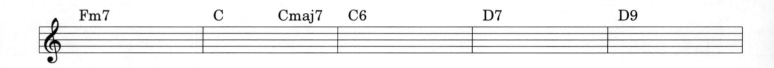

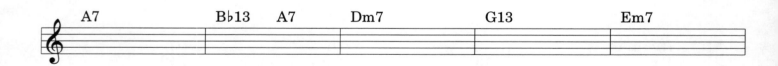

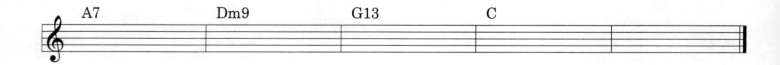

Bass-String Chords (ala Freddy Green)

Another type of dead-string chord is the *bass-string chord*. These chords are commonly used by guitarists who play in big bands. The great jazz guitarist Freddy Green (who played for years with The Count Basie Orchestra) was very fond of using these chords. Like dead-string chords, there are two categories of bass-string chords — those with the root on the sixth string and those with the root on the fifth string.

Drawn on the diagrams below are the most frequently used bass-string chords.

First Category
(Sixth String Root)

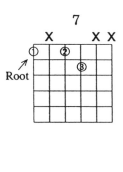
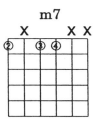
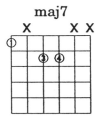
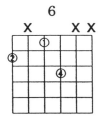

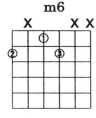
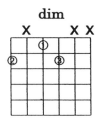
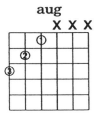

Practice the following progression which uses bass-string chords from the first category.

29

㉒

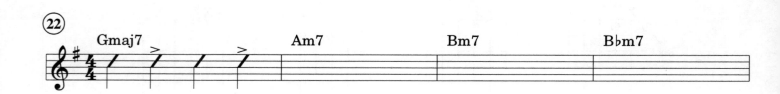

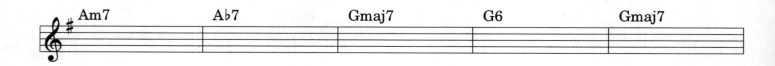

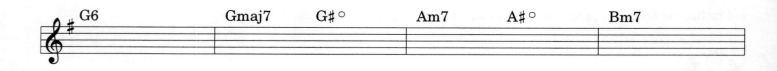

Second Category
(Fifth String Root)

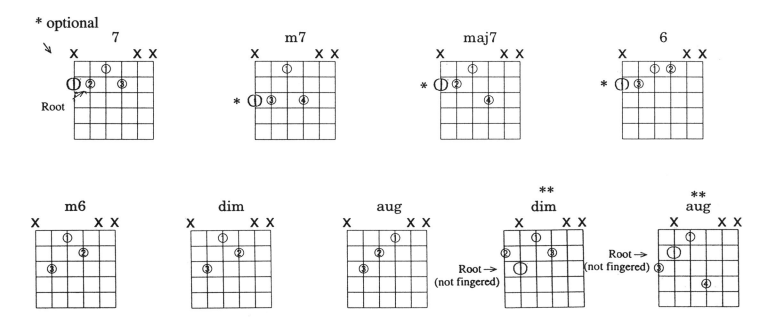

* The circle indicates the option of moving the finger which is on the fifth string, to the sixth string. If this is done, the fifth string should be dampened.

** If the option of placing a finger on the sixth string is used, these are the fingerings for the diminished and augmented chords. The root is located where the "R" is written on the fifth string.

11 Practice the following progression which uses bass-string chords from the second category.

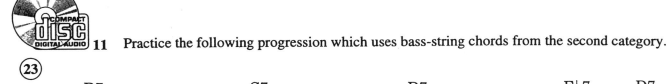

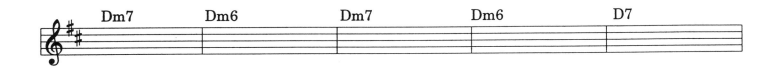

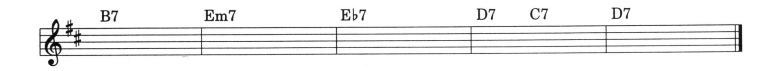

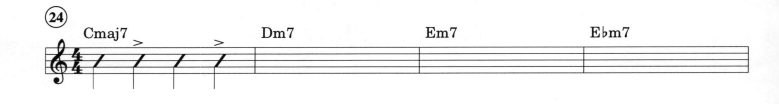

(24) Cmaj7 > > | Dm7 | Em7 | E♭m7

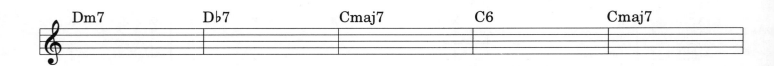

Dm7 | D♭7 | Cmaj7 | C6 | Cmaj7

C6 | Cmaj7 C#° | Dm7 D#° | Em7

E♭° | Dm7 | D♭7 | Cmaj7

The following progressions use bass-string chords from both categories. As with barre chords, combining the patterns from both categories makes it possible to keep the chords close to each other. This provides for good "voice leading." This means the notes in one chord lead smoothly to the notes in the next chord.

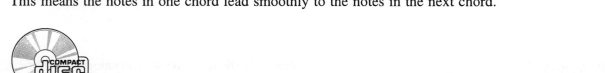

12

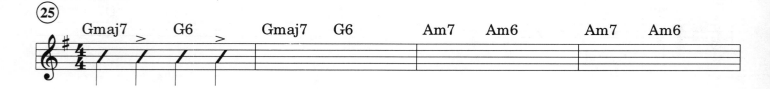

(25) Gmaj7 > G6 > | Gmaj7 G6 | Am7 Am6 | Am7 Am6

Gmaj7 G6 | Gmaj7 G6 | Bm7 | B♭m7

Am7 | D7 | Gmaj7 G6 | Gmaj7

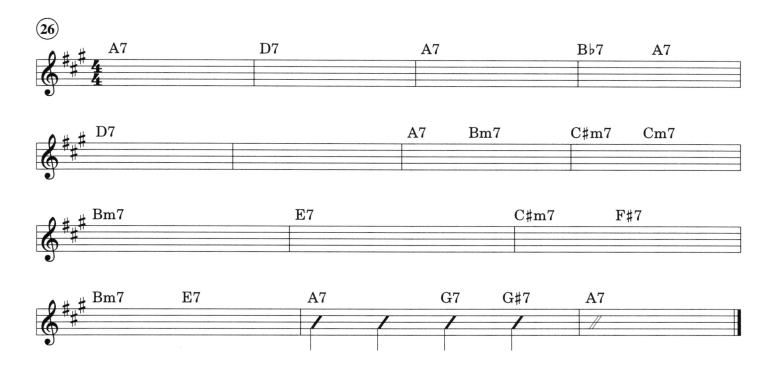

The next two progressions are a series of chords moving in fourths (each chord is four letter names up a scale from the preceding chord). Notice the left-hand third finger is a guide finger and connects one chord pattern to the next. When playing these exercises, the guide finger should slide along the string, but not lift off as the chords change.

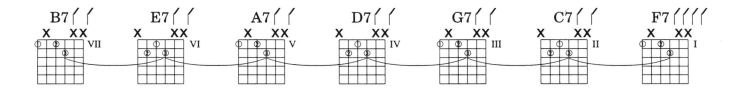

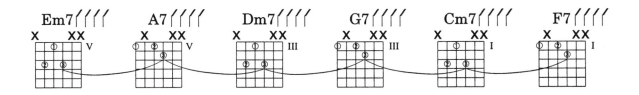

When using bass-string chords, if the written chord is not maj7, 7, m7, 6, or m6, reduce (or modify) the written chord to one of those chords and use a bass-string chord. For example, if the written chord is C7♭9♯5, you could reduce it to C7 and use a bass-string chord. For B♭, you could play B♭maj7. The following chart shows which bass-string chords to use for other chord types which may be written.

For	Use
any chord (except 6th) from the major family (i.e. major, maj9, add9, 6/9, maj7♯11, etc.)	maj7
any chord (except m6) from the minor chord family (i.e. minor, m9, m7sus, etc.)	m7
any chord from the dominant seventh family (i.e. 7sus, 9, 11, 13, 7th with and altered fifth or ninth (i.e. 7♯5♭9)).	7
dim	dim
aug	aug
6 and Major chords	6
m6	m6

In the following example, the chords on the bottom are what you might typically see in a jazz rhythm guitar part. The chords written on the top are the bass-string chords which could be used. Practice the progression using bass-string chords.

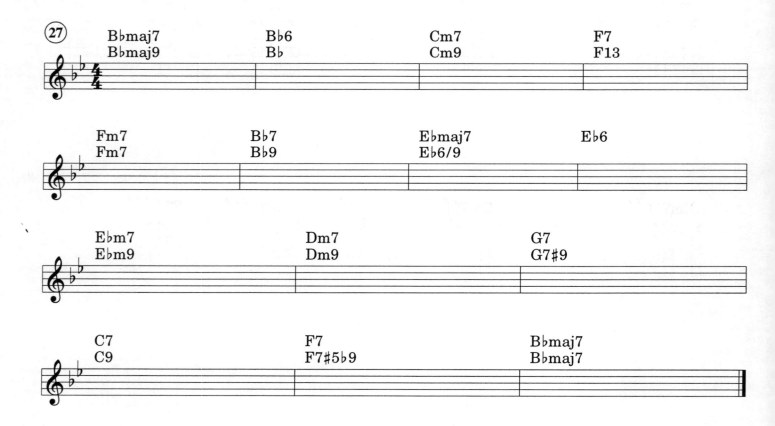

Comping

Comping is a term which is short for accompaniment. It usually refers to short rhythm patterns such as this:

. These comp patterns can be combined and are commonly used for playing accompaniment in jazz guitar. Written below are many comp patterns which will work for 4/4, 3/4, 6/8, 12/8, 5/4, and 7/4. Each pattern takes one or two measures to complete and can be used to accompany any music in those meters. Once you have selected a pattern to use, you can use the same pattern in each measure of the piece, or combine some of the patterns from the same meter. Hold any chord and practice each pattern. Be careful to use the correct strum direction and count the rhythm. Except for Latin rhythms, these patterns should be played using swing rhythm. If you don't know how to play swing rhythm, refer to the section in this book on page 11.

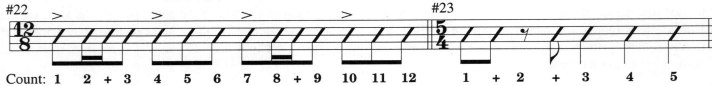

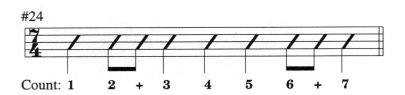

Each pattern can be played several times in succession, or the patterns can be combined.

Practice comping the following progressions. In each measure of the progression, use the pattern which is written in the first one or two measures. Then, practice using another comp patterns to play the same progression.

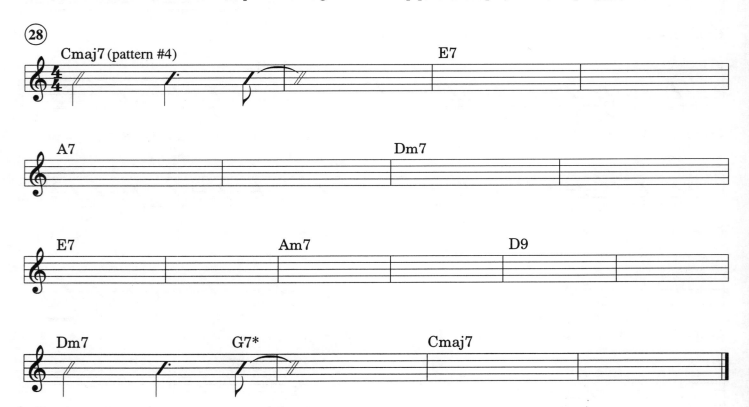

*If a two-measure comp pattern has a tie or a rest in the second measure, and the chord changes in the middle of the pattern, play the second chord on the "and" of 4 in the first measure of the pattern.

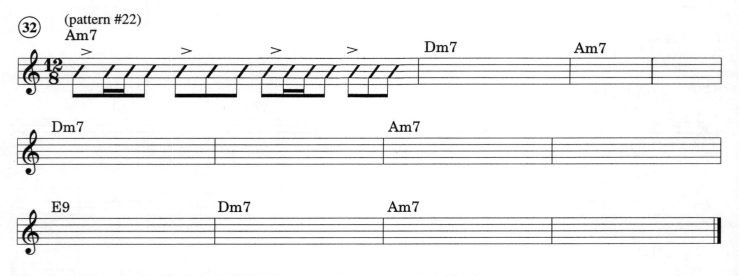

The next two examples show how different comp patterns can be combined.

Use the comp patterns from this section of the book to play the rhythm parts for the examples in this book. Also, go back and play some of the exercises from the earlier sections using comp patterns.

Chord Inversions (Four-String Chords)

A *chord inversion* is one which does not have the root on the bottom (the lowest note). The chords presented here are played on the first four strings of the guitar so they are often referred to as *four-string chords*. An "R" has been written on the diagram next to a dot showing where the root is located in the chord. Notice that some of the patterns <u>do</u> have the root as the lowest note in the chord. These chord patterns are in *root position*. The other patterns are inversions. Knowing these patterns will give you several ways to play every chord. A knowledge of these patterns will also be very helpful in building chord melodies and soloing.

The patterns are grouped by chord type. To find a particular chord, position the correct pattern for the type of chord so that the root is in the fret naming the chord.

The chart below shows the location of the notes for finding the roots on the first four strings.

Fret Number – – – – –	0	1	2	3	4	5	6	7	8	9	10	11	12
Notes on the 1st string	E	F		G		A		B	C		D		E
Notes on the 2nd string	B	C		D		E	F		G		A		B
Notes on the 3rd string	G		A		B	C		D		E	F		G
Notes on the 4th string	D		E	F		G		A		B	C		D

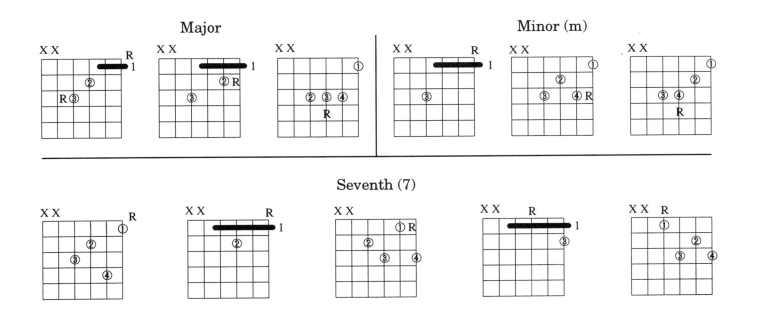

Major Seventh (maj7)

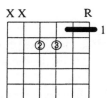 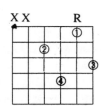 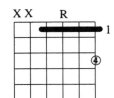 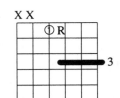 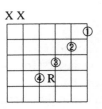

Minor Seventh (m7)

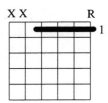 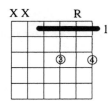 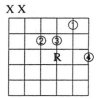 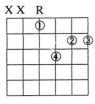

Sixth (6)	Diminished (○)	Augmented (+)

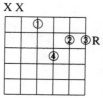 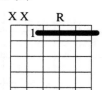 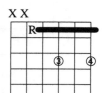   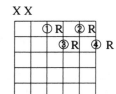   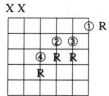

Minor Sixth (m6)

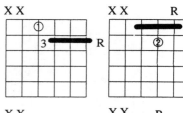

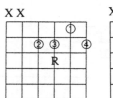 

Minor Major Seventh (m+7)

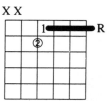

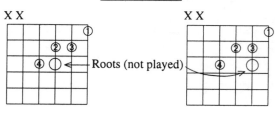

Roots (not played)

Suspended (sus)

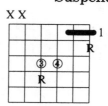 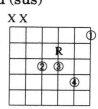

Add Nine (add9)

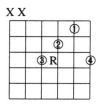 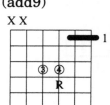

The three patterns below show where the three forms of the F (major) chord would be played. These are all F chords because the root of each chord is an F note.

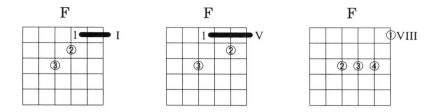

Practice the following progressions using four-string chords. The patterns have been drawn above the measures to help you. Notice that by using four-string chords the chords can be kept close together. Strum four times in a measure, or use comp patterns.

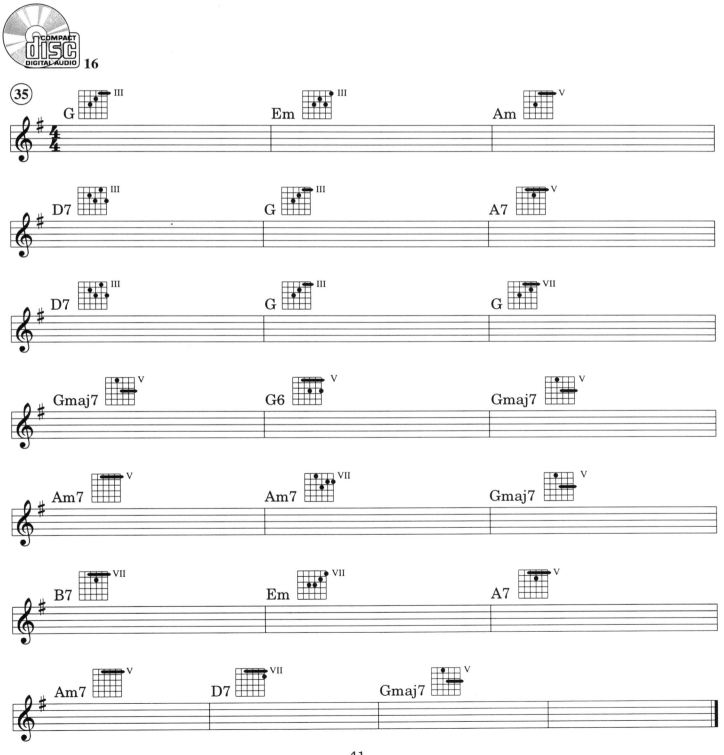

41

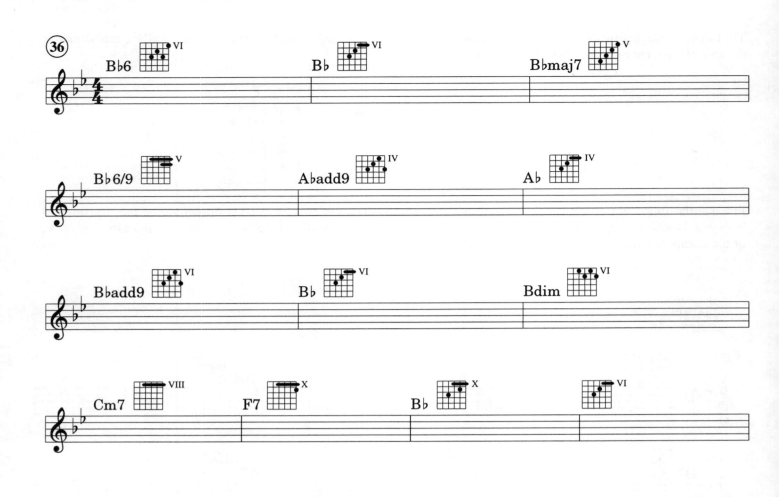

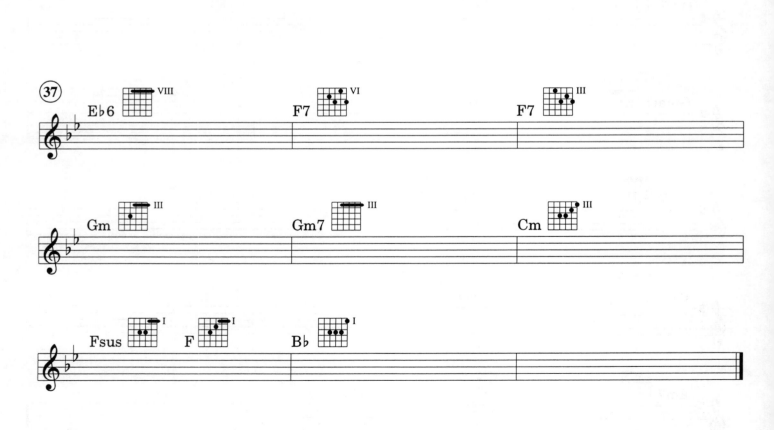

Play the following progressions using four-string chords of your choice. The same progression can be played several ways. Practice playing the progression several times. Each time, use a different chord pattern for the first chord. Then, try to keep the other chords in the same area. If the same chord is played for more than one measure, you can play the same chord form for both measures or play the same chord using a different pattern for the second measure.

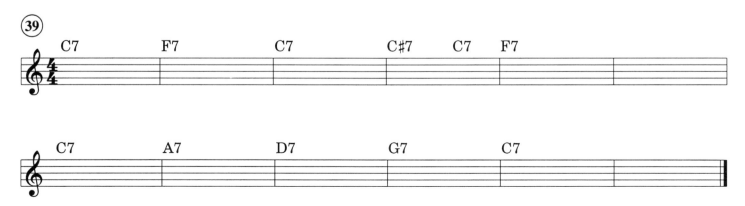

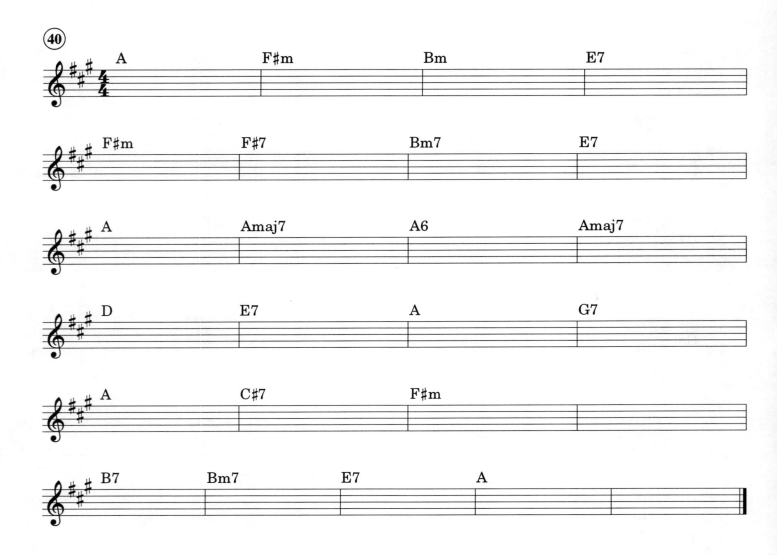

A good exercise to practice would be to play songs you know, only play the chords as four-string chords. They may sound a little thin compared to what you're used to hearing, but they are very valuable both for rhythm and solo playing. When playing rhythm guitar, four-string chords are very useful if you are playing with another guitarist or a keyboard player.

Altered Seventh Chords

An *altered chord* is one in which some of the notes (intervals) in the chord have been raised or lowered. Some common fingerings for altered chords are drawn below. Sharp and/or flat signs written before numbers indicate how to alter the interval. Altered intervals can also be indicated with a dash or a plus sign. A dash (-) before a 5 or 9 indicates a flat. A plus sign (+) before a 5 or 9 indicates a sharp. For example, C7+9-5 indicates C seven, sharp nine, flat five. This chord: D7+5-9 is a D7 sharp five, flat nine. An augmented seventh chord is written as: 7+ or +7. This means to play a seventh chord with a raised fifth. It can also be written as 7+5.

Drawn on the diagrams below are some of the more common altered seventh chords.

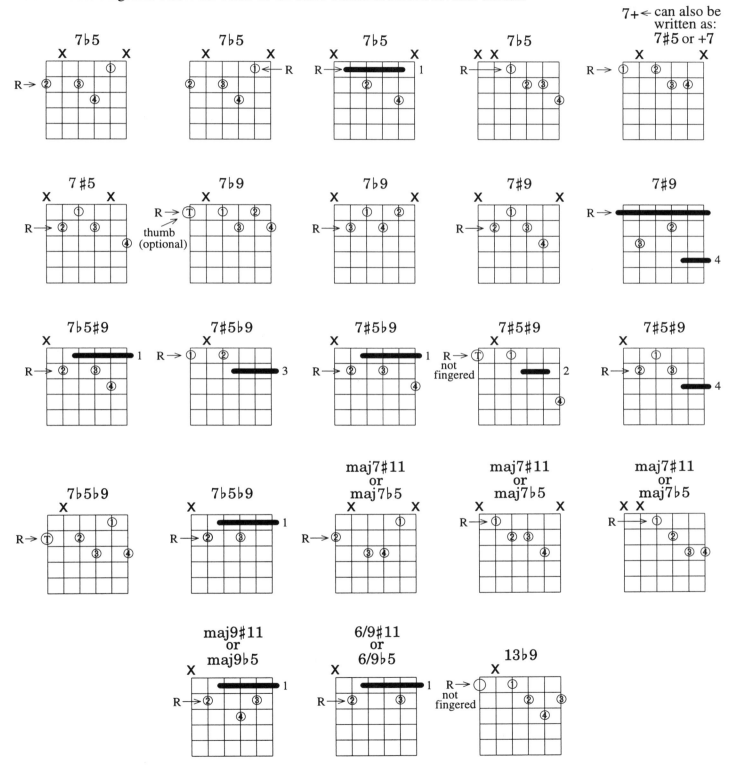

45

Practice the following progressions which contain altered chords. Strum down four times in a measure or use comp patterns.

18

(41)

Dm7	G7#5	C	
Dm7	G7+(same as 7#5)	Cmaj7	
Dm7	G7#5♭9	Cmaj7	Dm7
G7#9	Cmaj7	Em7	Am7
D7♭5	Gmaj7	Am7	D7♭9
Gmaj7		D7#9	Gmaj7
Am7	D7♭5♭9	G	
Am7	D7♭5#9	G	Gmaj7
Am7	D9	Gmaj7#11	Gmaj7
Dm7	G7	C6/9#11	C6/9

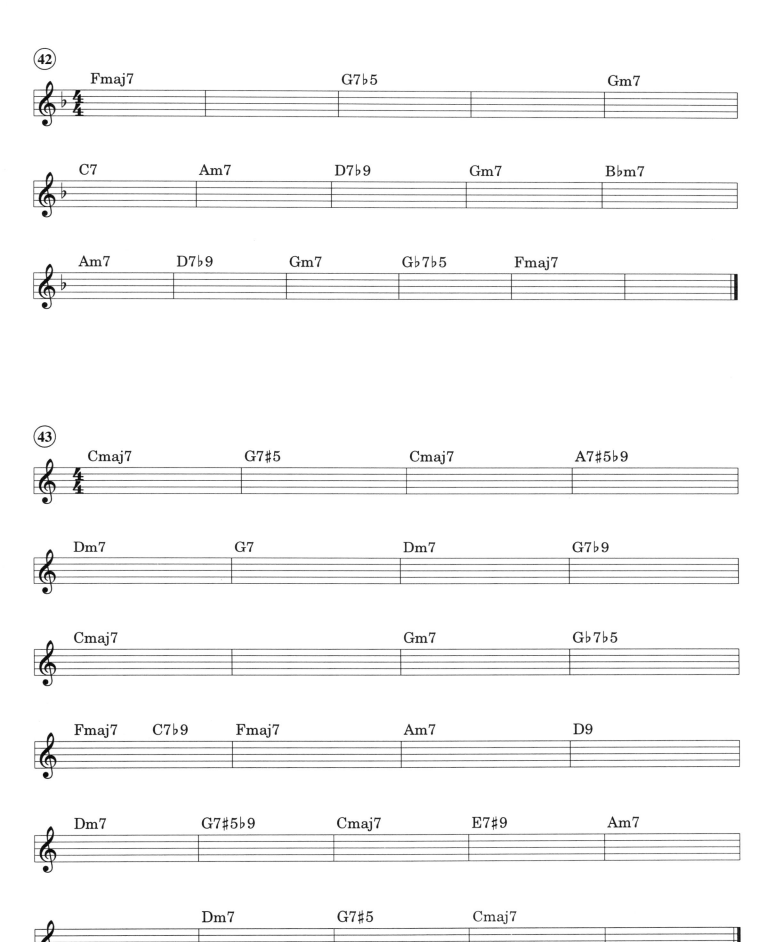

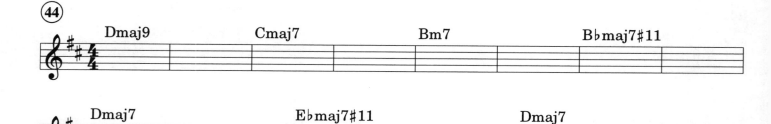

Altered chords commonly occur on the dominant seventh (7) chord (i.e., 7#9). The intervals which are usually altered in the seventh chords are the fifth and ninth. This is done to create a stronger "pull" to the next chord. Altered chords have a dissonance which is resolved by the chord which follows after the altered chord. Rather than memorizing patterns for the various types of altered dominant seventh chords, you will probably remember them better if you build your own. To find the fingering for a particular altered chord, start with the seventh chord form such as the one drawn below.

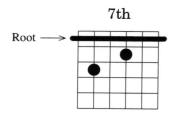

Next locate the interval in the chord which is going to be altered. For example, if you wanted to build a G7#5 chord, start with the fingering of a basic G7 chord and locate the interval of the fifth in the chord (the location of the intervals in the chord forms will be shown to you later in this section).

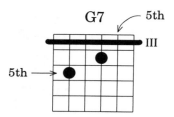

Next, sharp the fifth and add that note into the basic G7 chord. It's important to know that **altered intervals are never doubled in the chord.** For example in a 7#5 chord, only one #5 is played. The other 5th is omitted. Another example would be if the 9th is flatted, play only one flat 9th in the chord. Do not play any other 9th in the chord. Also, **it's best to place the altered intervals on the high strings of the chord (strings one, two, or three).**

Drawn below is the fingering you would end up with for G7#5.

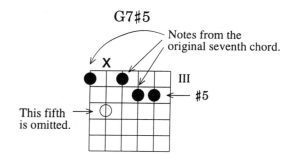

If you wanted to build a G7♭9 chord, begin with the fingering for a G7 and find the ninths which are located by the chord form.

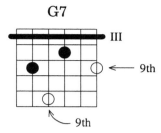

Next, flat the ninth and add it into the G7 chord. Remember to omit the lower ninth.

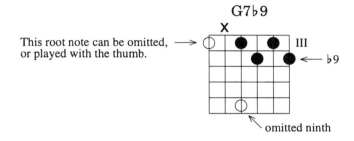

Drawn on the diagram below is the fingering of a seventh chord with the root on the sixth string. Also, indicated on the diagram are the locations of the intervals of a fifth and ninth. On the blank diagrams, draw the altered chords whose names are written above each diagram. All of these altered chords are built by adding altered intervals to the pattern of the 7th chord which is drawn below.

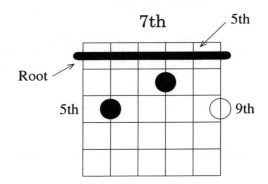

7#5   7♭5   7#9   7♭9   7#5♭9   7#5#9

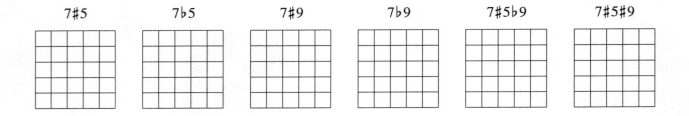

The following diagram shows the fingering of another 7th chord form and the location of the 5ths and 9ths. On the diagrams below the 7th chord, draw the altered chords.

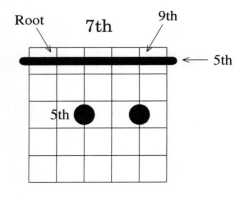

7♭5   7#5#9

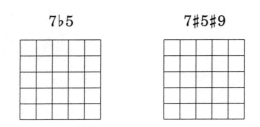

Drawn below is a third form of a 7th chord and the locations of the 5th and 9th intervals are shown. In the blank diagrams below the chord form, draw the altered chords.

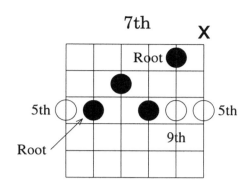

7♭5

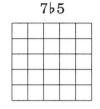

7♭9

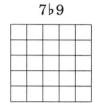

7♯9

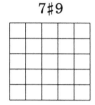

7♭5♭9

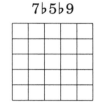

7♭5♯9

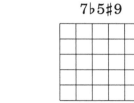

7♯5♯9

7♯5♭9

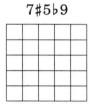

The location of the chord before the altered chord will determine which of the altered chord patterns is used. Try to keep the chord changes convenient and close to each other. Practice playing the following progressions which contain altered chords you have constructed. Strum down four times in each measure or use the comp patterns you have learned.

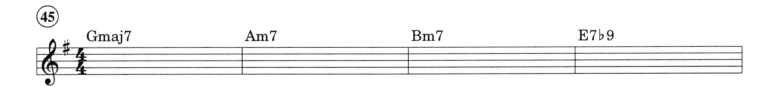

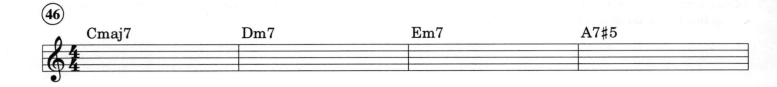

The real art in using altered chords is not so much in playing the chords themselves, but resolving them correctly. That is, making sure that the altered chord is followed by the correct chord so that the voicing of the altered chord resolves correctly.

To resolve the altered chords correctly, the flatted intervals in the altered chord (♭5) should resolve down one half step (one fret) on the next chord, and sharped intervals (♯9) should resolve up one half step in the chord which follows the altered chord. The diagrams below show examples of how altered chords should resolve.

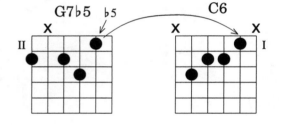

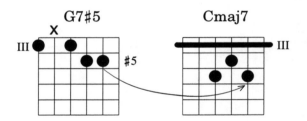

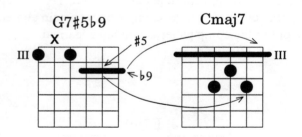

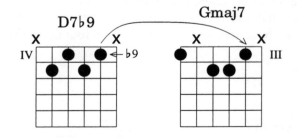

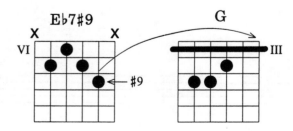

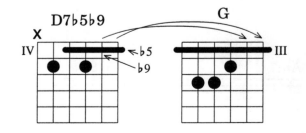

Practice playing the following progressions which contain altered chords and illustrate how the chords are resolved.

Major Scales

To better understand string soloing and improvisation, it is important to have a working knowledge of major scales. Major scales are the basis for understanding the other scales and modes you will be learning. The major scale is constructed with a whole step (two frets), whole step, half step (one fret), whole step, whole step, whole step, and a half step. No matter what note you begin on, if you follow this formula, you will have a major scale. Written below are the C major and D major scales. Notice that the C major scale has no sharps or flats and that the D major scale has an F♯, and a C♯. In the D scale, the F and C must be sharp so the notes fit the major scale formula.

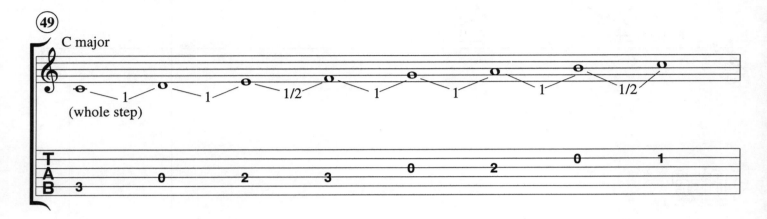

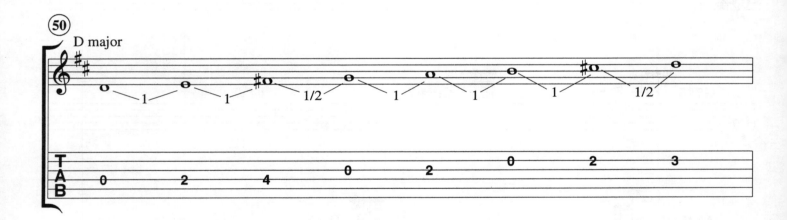

Six fingering diagrams for the major scales are shown on the next page. The location of the roots are indicated with a diamond. The black numbers in the circles are also notes in the major scale, but they are the extended notes above and/or below the octave. Some of the patterns have the roots on the sixth string and others have the roots on the fifth string. With all of the scales in this book, first practice each of the scale patterns beginning with the lowest root (indicated with a diamond) and play to the highest root in the pattern. Second, practice the patterns beginning with the lowest root and playing to the highest note in the pattern (playing the notes which may go above the octave and are written as black circled numbers). Finally, play the patterns including the notes which go below and above the octave(s). Practice the scales by playing the notes in the scale in order from low to high. Then, reverse the order. Finally, practice mixing up the notes of the scale in any order you like.

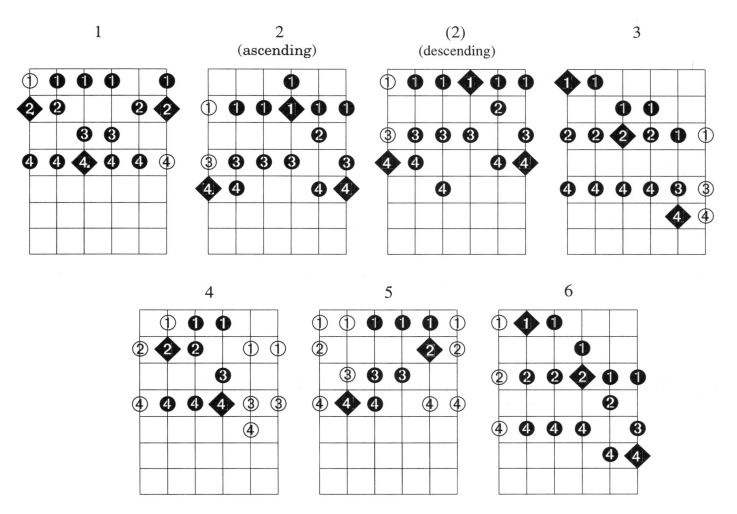

Many of the scale patterns in the book are vertical scales. That is, they run straight across the guitar neck. By connecting these vertical patterns to one another, the vertical patterns can become horizontal. The following diagram illustrates one way in which two vertical major scale patterns can be connected on the fourth string to become a horizontal pattern. The circled area shows the resulting horizontal scale pattern. The scale patterns can be connected on any string. Play one scale pattern up to a certain string, then shift on that string to the next pattern. Don't be afraid to experiment.

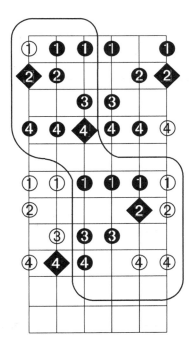

Practice the following solo which is in the key of G and uses notes from the G major scale (pattern number one with the root on the sixth string, third fret).

After you can play the exercises and solos as written in this book, **practice transposing the same exercises and solos in several different keys.**

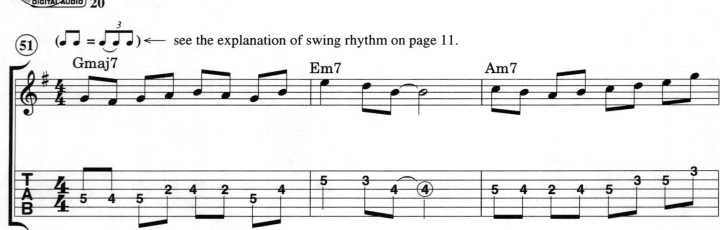

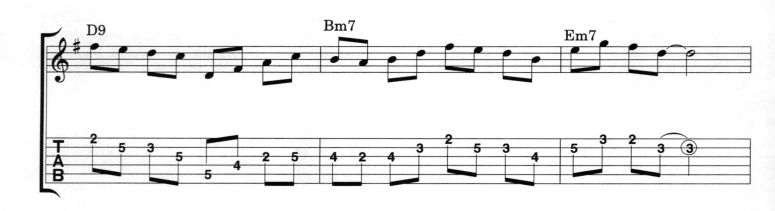

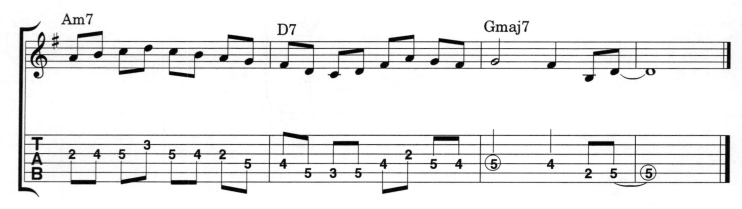

Practice the next solo which is in the key of C and use the C major scale (pattern number two with the root on the fifth string, third fret).

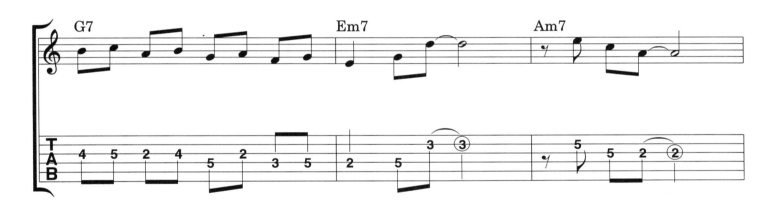

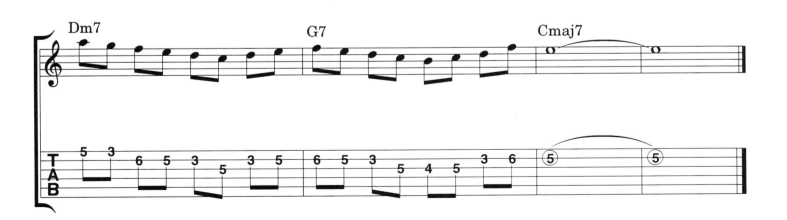

Above each of the following progressions is written the name of the major scale which can be used to improvise over the entire progression. The number written by the name of the key indicates which major scale fingering from page 55 to use. If you have the recording which goes with this book, practice playing the scale with the progressions which is played on the recording. If you don't have the recording, record the chord progression yourself, play it back and practice playing the scales to the progressions. At first, simply play the scales down and back. Then, practice mixing up the notes of the scale. Remember to use the same major scale for the entire progression. Practice each example separately, then connect by going from one to the next. As you go from one progression to the next, remember the major scale which is used must change for each progression. For example, in the first example use the C major scale, then for the next progression use the D major scale. This will give you a chance to practice combining the different scale patterns.

 21

(53) CMajor #2

| Dm7 | G7 | Dm7 | G7 | Cmaj7 | |

DMajor #4

| Em7 | A7 | Em7 | A7 | Dmaj7 | |

FMajor #5

| Gm7 | C7 | Gm7 | C7 | Fmaj7 | |

B♭Major #1 or #3

| Cm7 | F7 | Cm7 | F7 | B♭maj7 | |

Tonal Centers (Major)

Although you were not aware of it, at the end of the last section you were using *tonal centers*. Tonal center is a term which means identifying the name of the key from the chords that are being played. Using tonal centers means you will be playing the major scale which had the same letter name as the key. If the key changes, you change the scale to match the name of the key. **You can't trust the key signature.** In some styles, it is very common for the piece to stay in the same key. But in jazz, it is common for the key to change in the piece and not be indicated in the key signature. The key can be identified by looking at the key signature, but very often in jazz it is better to find the key by looking at the chords and determining which key contains those chords. You have to be able to identify the key (tonal center) by the chords which are being played. Eventually, your ear can pick up on these key changes without having to see them written. In order to find the key of a song (or a portion of a song), you have to know the chords which are in that key. One way of locating the key (tonal center) is to use the chord clock which is drawn below. All of the basic chords appear on the clock. To find the six basic chords in any given key, look at the key chord (the chord which has the same letter name as the key); then take the chords which are clockwise and counterclockwise of that chord and the three chords which are connected to them on the inside of the clock. This will give you the six basic chords in the key. On the clock below, circles have been placed around the chords in the keys of G and E. If a progression uses a chord other than these six, the progression is going into a new key.

If a chord in the progression is not on the clock, reduce it to one which is. For example, Fm7 could be reduced to Fm. G7 could be reduced to G, and Cmaj7 reduced to C.

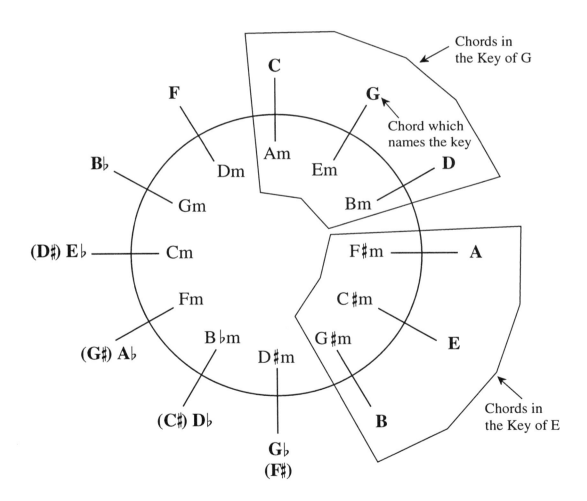

A good signal to look for in finding tonal centers is the seventh (7) chord. A seventh will only appear on the V chord. This is the chord which letter name is five steps up the major scale of the key. This chord is just clockwise of the key on the chord clock. For example, if you see G7, you are most likely in the key of C and should be using the C scale to improvise. A minor chord used in the progression may signal the use of the ii chord. The ii chord is one whole step above the name of the key. For example, the ii chord in the key of C is Dm. However, minor chords may also be vi chords or iii chords. If the minor chord is followed by a seventh chord, it (the minor chord) is most likely the ii chord. You could play the major scale with the letter name of the I (key) chord for the improvisation. Remember, the I chord is one whole step (two frets) below the ii chord.

In the following progression, the key changes several times. Brackets have been placed around the sections that are in each key, and written in the brackets above the chords is the name of the key for that particular section of the progression. To improvise over this progression, in each separate section of the progression, play the major scale which has the same letter name as that portion of the music. If the key changes, and you were to use the same scale throughout the entire progression, it wouldn't work. By changing the scales, and having them match the keys, the scales fit the chords. If you don't have the recording which goes with this book, record yourself or have another guitarist play the chords for you while you practice improvising using the tonal center concept.

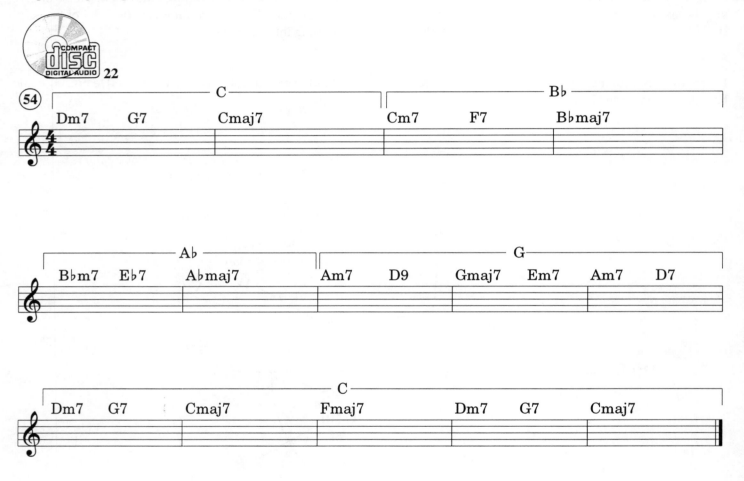

The next solo changes key several times. The name of the key for each section has been written in brackets above the chords. The name of the key written in the brackets is the letter name of the major scale which should be used for the solo in that section of the music. Practice this solo and then try making up your own solo to the same chords.

It's important to notice that although one scale is being used over an entire section of music, a chord tone (a note in the chord) is being played on heavy beats (beats one and three in 4/4 and beat one in 3/4). These chord tones are easily located on the guitar by simply looking at the notes which are played when a particular chord is fingered.

Find the tonal centers in the following progressions. You can circle them or write the name of the key in brackets above the chords. It's very common for jazz standards to change keys in the song. If you have a fake book (and you should), locate the tonal centers (key changes) in some of the standard tunes.

The m7♭5 Chord

The m7♭5 chord is a type of altered chord. The m7♭5 chord can also be written as m7-5. It is also sometimes called a half diminished chord which is written like this: ø. The m7♭5 chord often appears as the ii chord in a minor key. Drawn below are the three most common fingerings for the m7♭5 chord. One has the root on the sixth string, one on the fifth, and one on the fourth string.

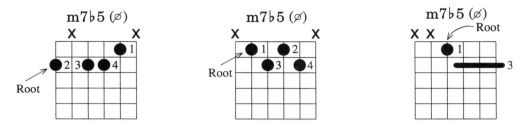

Practice each of the following progressions which contain m7♭5 chords. Use the fingerings which are drawn next to the chord names. As with the other altered chords, resolve the ♭5 down one half step (one fret) on the chord which follows the m7♭5.

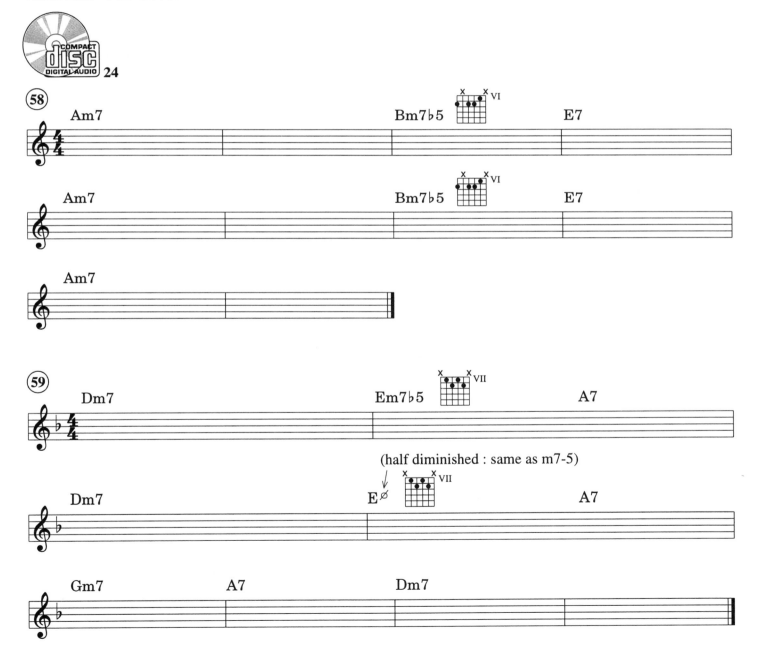

63

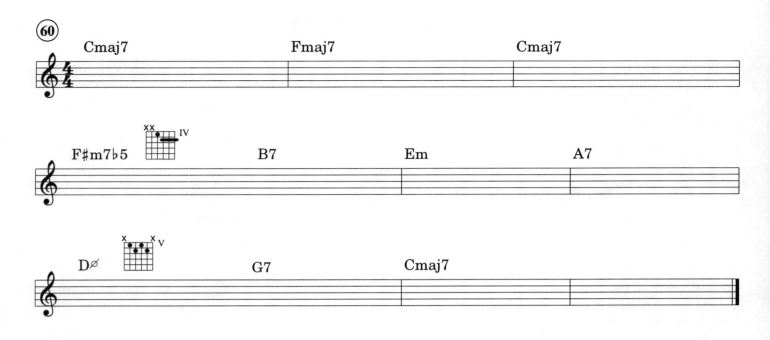

The major scale can be used to improvise over the m7♭5 chord. To do this, use the major scale which is 1/2 step (one fret) higher than the letter name of the m7♭5 chord. For example, over a Bm7♭5 chord you can play the C major scale. In the following example, the F major scale is used over the Em7♭5 chord.

25

(♩♩ = ♩♩♩) ← see the section in this book on "Swing Rhythm"

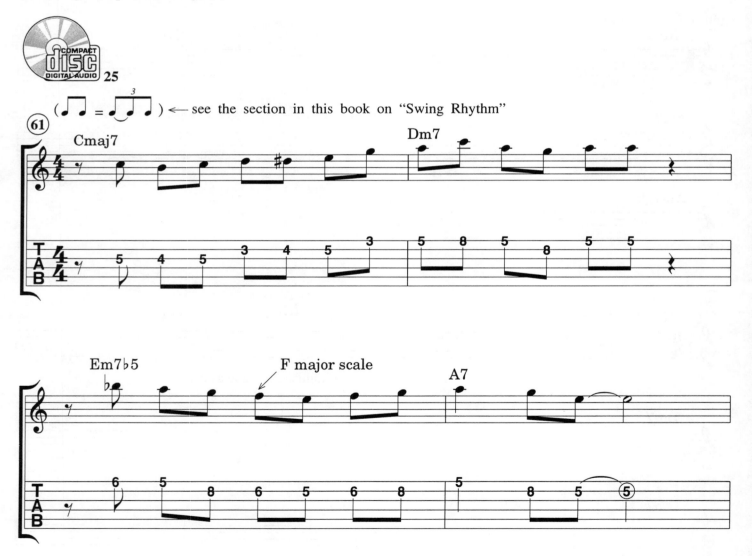

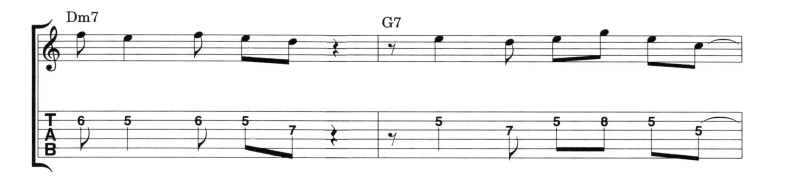

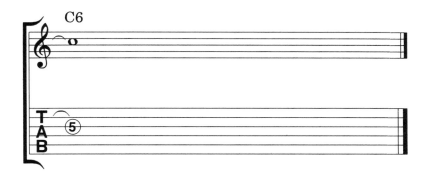

Another scale which is commonly used to improvise over the m7♭5 chord is the harmonic minor. This scale and its uses will be presented in the section of this book which deals with "Minor Scales."

Minor Scales

Minor scales are another important tool in improvisation. These scales are used to improvise in minor keys. In this section of the book there will be three minor scales presented and used: natural minor, harmonic minor, and melodic minor. The natural minor scale is built by taking the major scale and lowering the 3rd, 6th, and 7th degrees. Written below is the C natural minor scale.

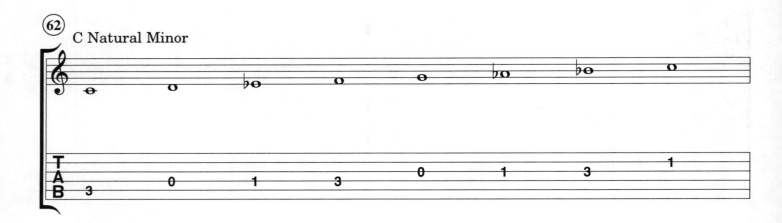

The following diagrams show the moveable fingerings for the natural minor scale. Notice that some of the patterns have the roots on the sixth string and some have the root on the fifth string.

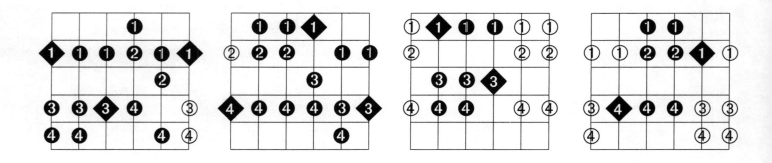

66

The natural minor scale can be used to improvise to minor type chords. The following example illustrates the use of natural minor scales with minor chords. The scale which is used for this solo is A natural minor. After practicing this solo, try improvising your own solo to the same chords using the A natural minor scale.

The harmonic minor scale is the natural minor scale with a raised seventh degree. This scale is very popular in jazz. It can be used to improvise to a single minor chord, or an entire minor chord progression. Written below are the C and A harmonic minor scales.

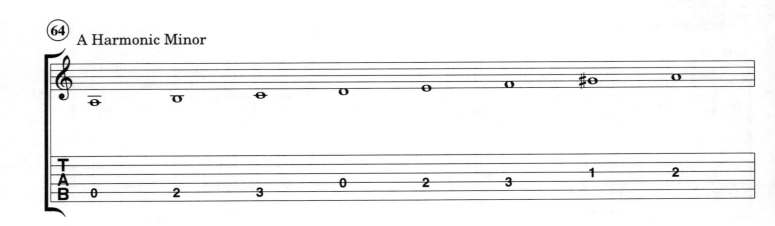

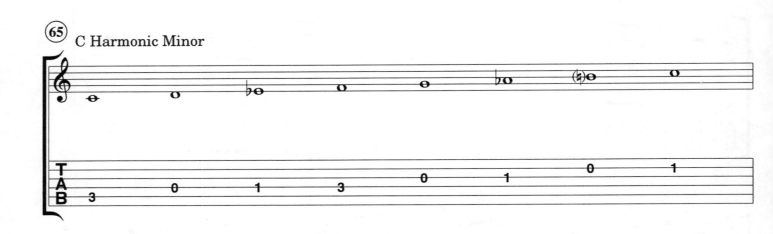

The following diagrams show the moveable fingerings for the harmonic minor scale.

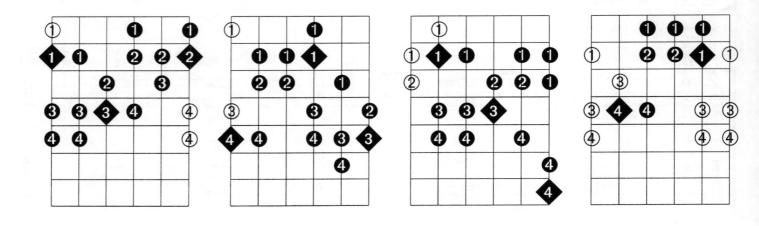

68

The next example shows how the harmonic minor scale is used with minor chords and minor chord progressions. This solo uses the D harmonic minor scale.

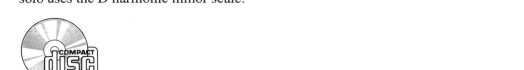

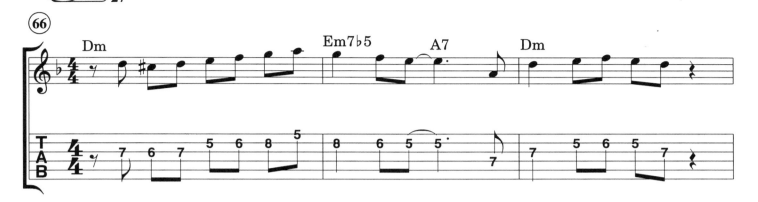

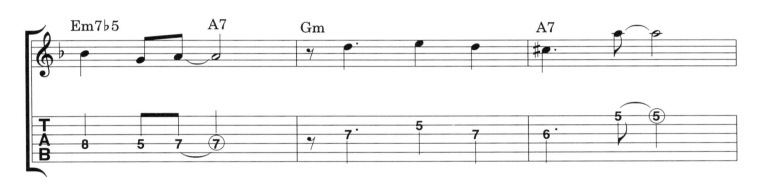

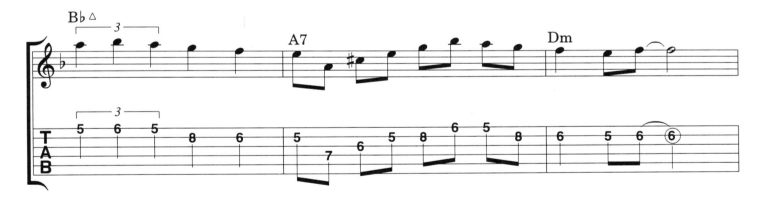

You can also use the harmonic minor scale to improvise over the m7b5 chord. You can play the harmonic minor scale which is one whole step below the letter name of the m7b5 chord. For example, over a Bm7b5 chord you can play the A harmonic minor scale. Using the harmonic minor scale in this manner is a very common practice in jazz. In the following solo, the A harmonic minor scale is used for the solo over the entire progression including the Bm7b5 chord.

In the next example, the harmonic minor scale one whole step below the m7♭5 chord has been used for the solo.

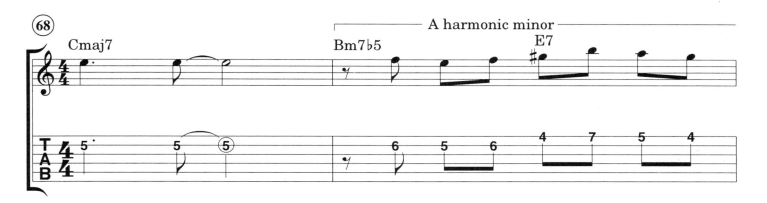

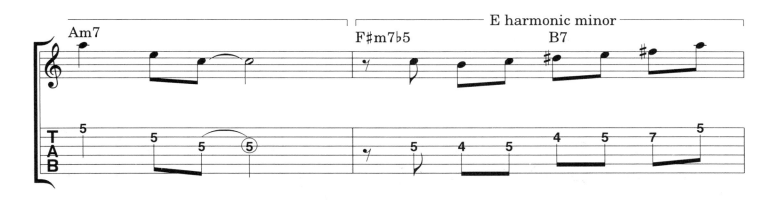

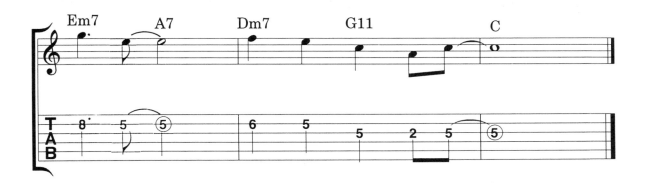

The melodic minor scale is made by taking the natural minor scale and raising the sixth and seventh degrees when ascending. When descending, the sixth and seventh degrees are not raised but are the same as the natural minor scale. Written below is the A melodic minor scale.

69 A Melodic Minor

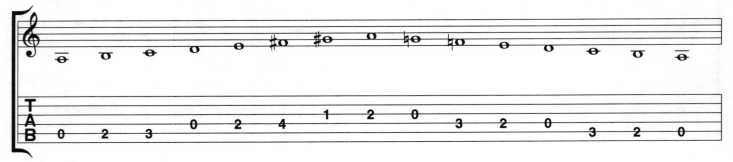

The diagrams below show the moveable fingerings for the melodic minor scale.

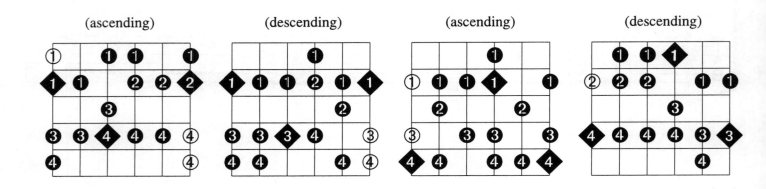

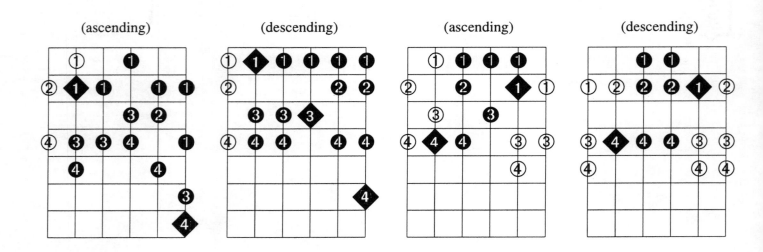

The following example shows how the melodic minor scale is used to play over minor chords and minor chord progressions. This next solo uses the A melodic minor scale.

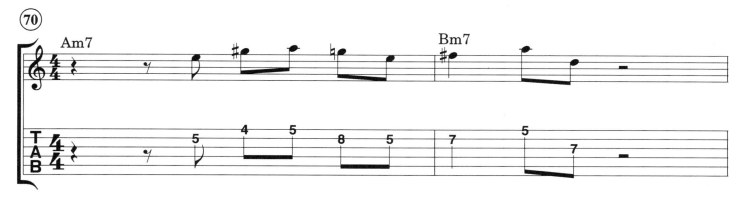

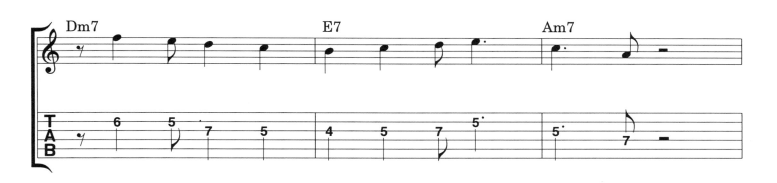

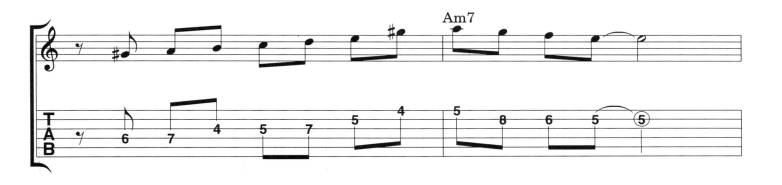

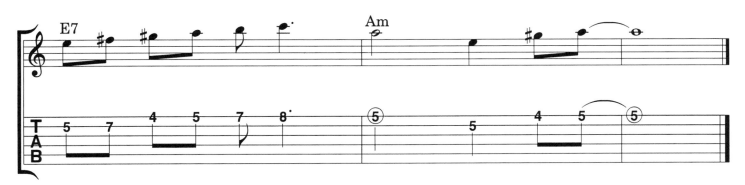

The jazz minor scale is similar to the melodic minor scale in that the 6th and 7th degrees are raised when ascending. It is different from the melodic minor scale in that when descending, the 6th and 7th degrees are still raised. Written below is the A jazz minor scale.

(71) A Jazz Minor

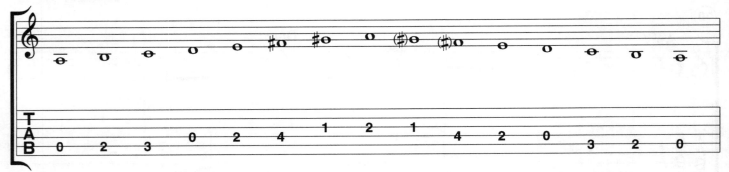

The moveable patterns for the jazz minor scale are drawn below.

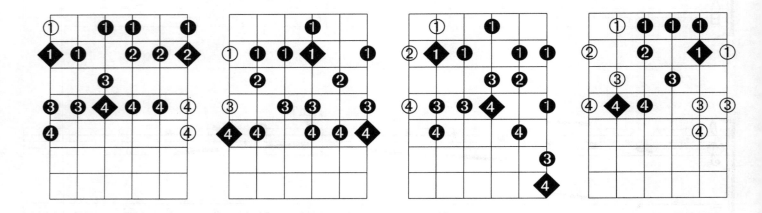

The next example illustrates the use of the E jazz minor scale.

Tonal Centers (Minor)

Remember, *tonal center* refers to finding the key. It is very common for a jazz piece to change key without the key change being indicated in the key signature. If you know what key the song (or a section of the song) is in, you can play the minor scale which has the same letter name as the key over several or all of the chords. This will work as long as the chords being played are all from the same minor key. Finding the tonal centers for minor keys can be done much the same as the major keys. Again, use the chord clock. Locate the key chord. Take that chord and the chords clockwise and counterclockwise of the key chord and the three chords on the outside of the clock which are connected to them. This is the same process that was used to find the chords in a major key, but now the primary chords are those on the inside of the clock. The difference in locating the chords in a minor key rather than a major key is, in a minor key, the chord just clockwise of the key chord is turned into a major (and usually a 7th) chord. On the chord clock below, the chords in the key of Am have been circled.

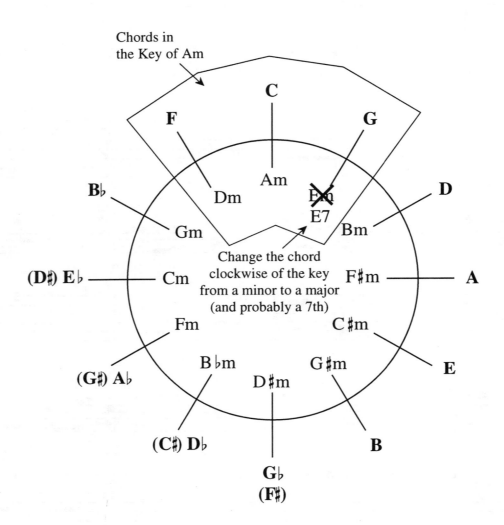

In a minor key, the most frequently used chords are the ones on the inside of the clock. For example in the key of Am, the most commonly used chords would be: Am, Dm and E7. If you are trying to find the chords to a song by ear and the song is in a minor key, try the chords from the key which are on the inside of the clock first. If they don't work, try the chords from the key which are on the outside of the clock.

Here are a few signals to watch for to determine if the chord progression is in a minor key.

1. If a 7th chord is followed by a minor or minor seventh chord, chances are that section of the song (or maybe the entire song) is in a minor key. For example, A7 to Dm is in the key of Dm. This would be a typical V-i progression. The D minor scale could be used to improvise to the entire progression.

2. The presence of a m7♭5 chord probably indicates a minor key because the ii chord in a minor key is often a m7♭5. For example, if you see a Bm7♭5 chord, you are probably in the key of Am (Bm7♭5 being the ii chord in the key of Am).

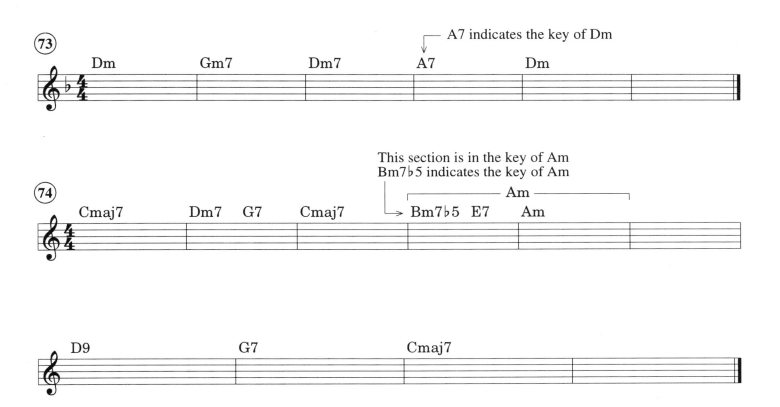

The following solo is in the key of Dm and uses the D harmonic minor scale. Practice this solo. Notice that the D harmonic minor scale has been used throughout the solo. As with using major tonal centers, one scale is used for the entire solo, and chord tones are played on heavy beats.

Here is a typical chord progression in the key of Am. Because all of the chords are in the key of Am, the Am scale can be used to improvise to the chords. If you have the recording which goes with this book, practice improvising a solo using the A minor scale. The type of minor scale you use is up to you. The harmonic minor scale would work well and is probably the most commonly used. If you don't have the recording, record yourself or have another guitarist or keyboard player play the chords while you improvise a solo using tonal centers.

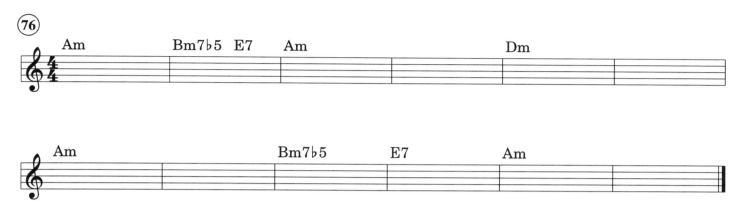

In the following solos, the key changes several times. The key changes have been indicated with brackets and the names of the keys are written in the brackets. Notice some sections are in major keys and some are in minor keys. The written solo changes scale each time the key changes. After you practice the written solo, make up your own solo to the same chords using the minor scales which have the same letter name as the keys. Use major scales in the major key sections and some type of minor scale (usually harmonic) over the minor key sections.

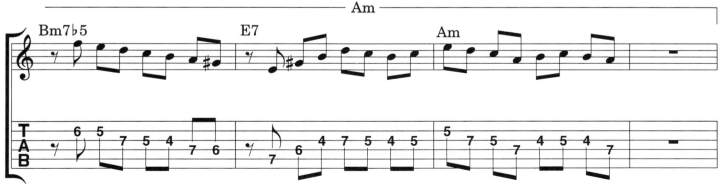

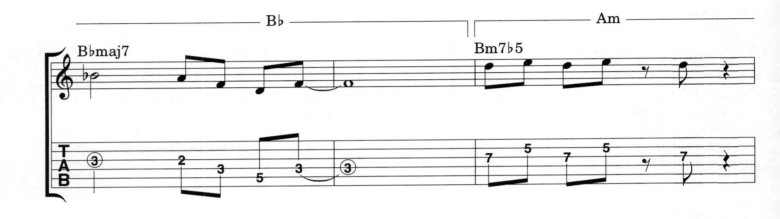

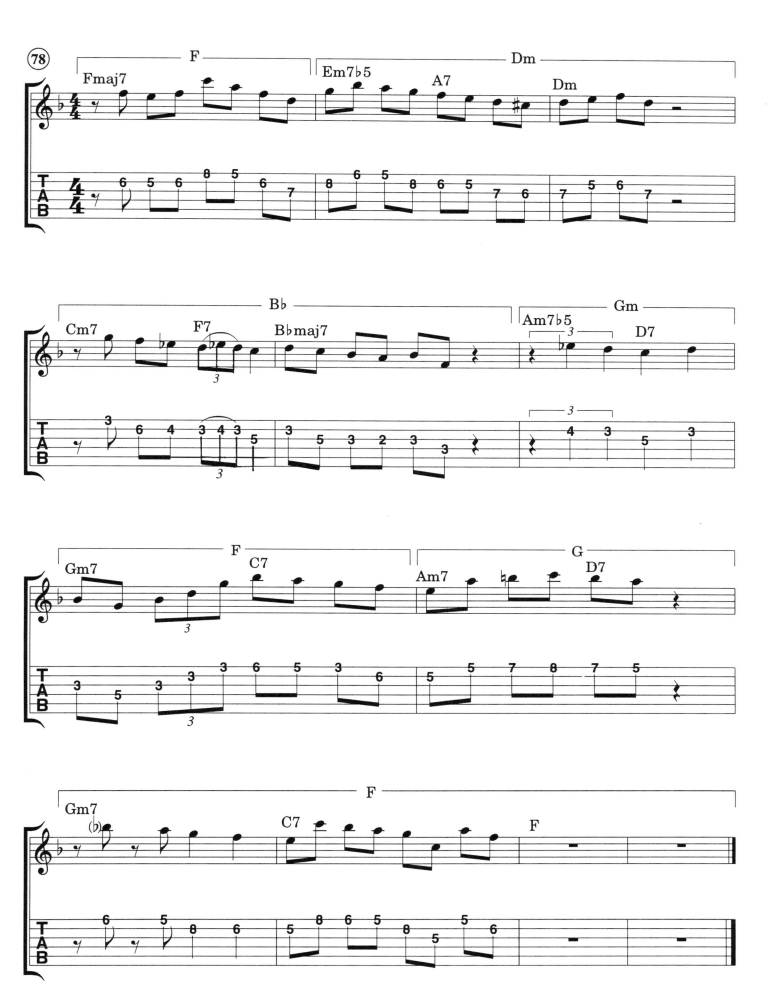

The following progression changes between minor and major. Practice improvising to these chords using the E harmonic minor and G major scales.

31

(79)
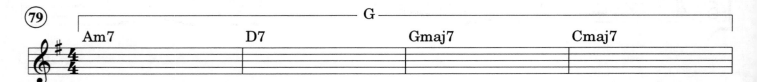

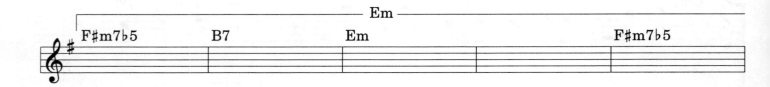

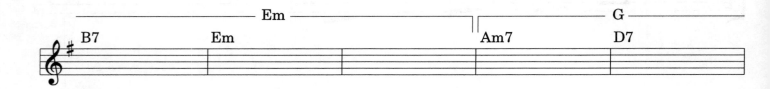

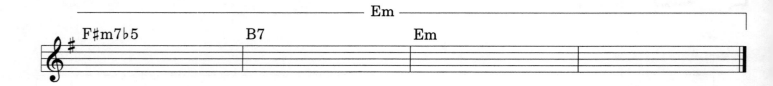

Chord Construction

A knowledge of how chords are built will be valuable in helping you to memorize chord forms and, later in this book, learning chord embellishment and chord substitution. On the following chart, the names of the various types of chords are written on the left, and the notes of the major scale which are used to build the chords are written to the right of the chord names. The major scale which is used to find the notes should have the same letter name as the chord. For example, a ninth chord contains a root (the note which names the chord), the third, fifth, flat seventh, and ninth steps of the major scale. The A9 chord would contain the following notes from an A major scale: A (root), C♯ (third), E (fifth), G (flat seventh) and B (ninth).

Some of the chords contain more notes than you have strings (or fingers). With these chords, some of the notes may have to be omitted. The numbers in parentheses under the notes in the chords indicate the order in which notes may be omitted so as to make the fingerings possible.

Abbreviations and chords symbols are used on the following chart. If you don't know the name of the chord for which the symbol is written, refer to the section at the beginning of this book on Chord Symbols and Abbreviations.

Major	root (note which has the same letter name as the name of the chord), 3, 5
minor	root, ♭3, 5
dim	root, ♭3, ♭5
aug	root, 3, ♯5
sus	root, 4, 5
6	root, 3, 5, 6
m6	root, ♭3, 5, 6
maj7	root, 3, 5, 7
maj7♯11	root, 3, 5, 7, ♯11 (♭5) (1)-*notes which can be omitted*
7	root, 3, 5, ♭7
+7 (7+)	root, 3, ♯5, ♭7
7sus	root, 4, 5, ♭7 (1)
m7	root, ♭3, 5, ♭7
m7sus	root, ♭3, 4, 5, ♭7 (1)
m+7	root, ♭3, 5, 7

m7♭5 (m7-5)	root, ♭3, ♭5, ♭7
maj9	root, 3, 5, 7, 9
maj9♯11 (maj9+11)	root, 3, 5, 7, 9 ♯11 (♭5) (1)
9	root, 3, 5, ♭7, 9 (1)
m9	root, ♭3, 5, ♭7, 9 (1)
add9	root, 3, 5, 9
6/9	root, 3, 5, 6, 9 (1)
6/9♯11 (6/9+11)	root, 3, 5, 6, 9, ♯11 (♭5) (1)
11	root, 3, 5, ♭7, 9, 11 (1)(2) (3)
13	root, 3, 5, ♭7, 9, 11, 13 (2) (3) (1)
7♭5 (7-5)	root, 3, ♭5, ♭7
7♯5 (7+5)	root, 3, ♯5, ♭7
7♭9 (7-9)	root, 3, 5, ♭7, ♭9 (1)
7♯9 (7+9)	root, 3, 5, ♭7, ♯9 (1)

Now that you can find the notes used to build the chords, if you know where those notes were located, you can construct the chord forms. The charts on the next three pages will help you to do just that. On each of the next three pages, a large diagram is drawn showing a fingering for a major chord (the heavy dark dots). The location of each of the notes, or intervals (i.e., 6th, 7th, 9th, etc.), from the major scale is shown around the major chord form. Start with the major chord form and then add the needed intervals to build the chord. For example, if I wanted to build an A13 chord, I would start with the A chord form:

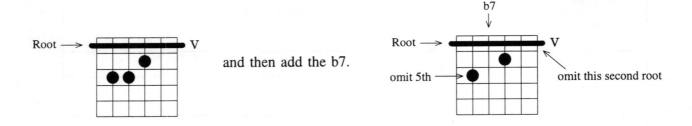

and then add the b7.

Finally, add the 13th.

So, A13 would look like this:

(the ninth can be omitted)

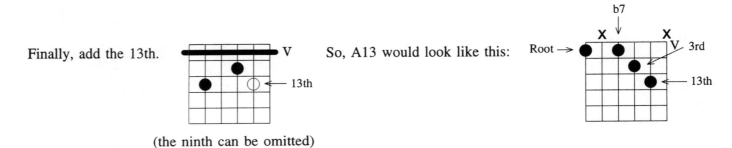

On the following diagram, the fingering of the major chord is indicated by the dots. The numbers show the location of the notes in the scale (intervals). Below each of the diagrams showing the intervals are several blank diagrams with chord names above them. Find and draw the fingering for each of those chords. You can check yourself by looking at the fingerings for these chords in the earlier sections of this book on barre chords, and dead string chords.

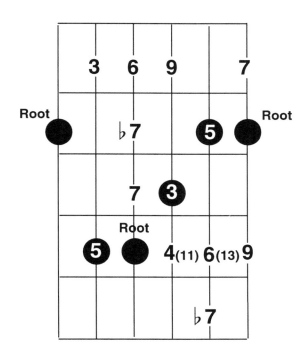

A9
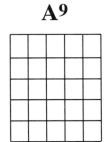

B♭13
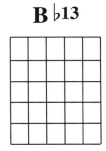

Gm9
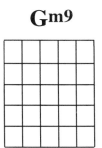

Bmaj7
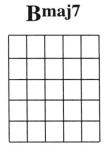

F♯7sus
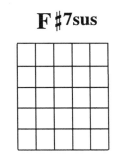

G7
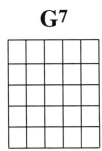

G7+9
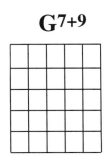

A♭7♯5
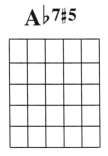

B♭m7
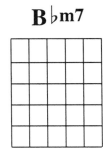

A6

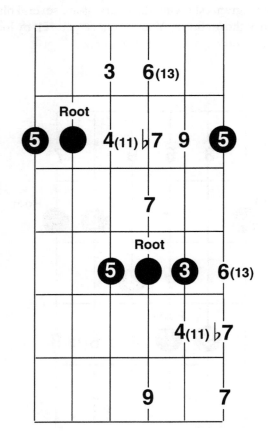

E♭maj7

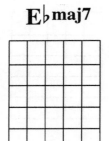

D6

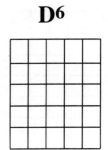

E add9

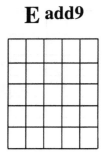

F7

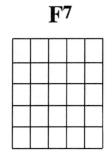

B♭7sus

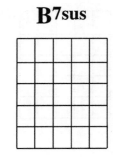

Cmaj7

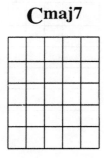

Cmaj9

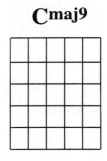

E♭6/9

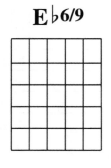

Dm7

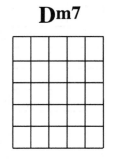

E♭7♭5

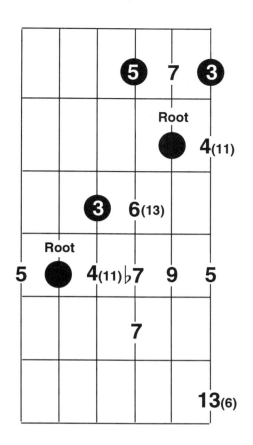

E♭maj7

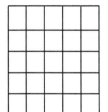

D7

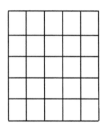

D6/9

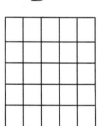

E11

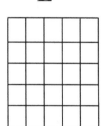

F6

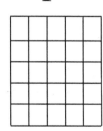

Dm9

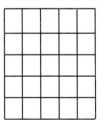

Cmaj9

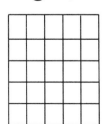

E7♯9

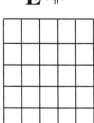

C7♭9♯5

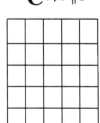

B7♭5♯9

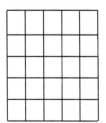

Practice the following progressions using chords you have constructed.

80
Gmaj7   Em7   Am7   D9   Gmaj7♯11   Gmaj7

F♯m7♭5   B7   Em   Em+7   Em7

Am7   Bm7   Am7   D11   G6/9

81
Cmaj9   Dm9   Cmaj9   G11

Dm7   G13   Cmaj9♯11   C6/9

E7   Bm7♭5   E7   Am   Am+7   Am7   Am6

Dm7   G7   Cmaj7

Connecting Chord Forms

The following exercises will help you learn to change chords smoothly by connecting the chord forms. By the time you finish these exercise you will be familiar with the chords most commonly used in jazz. The exercises are based on the ii-V-I chord progression.

To use the chart, play the chords from left to right. Play the chords in the left column for four beats, then the chords in the middle column for four beats, and finally, play the chords in the right column for eight beats. In some cases, the right column may beat split (four beats for each chord).

Root on 6th String	Root on 5th String	Root on 6th String	
Am	D	G	
Am7	D7	Gmaj7	
Am7	D7	Gmaj7	G6
Am7sus(Am11)	D7	G Gsus	G
Am9	D7sus D7sus D7	Gmaj9	
Am7	D9	Gmaj7	
Am7	D7	Gadd9	
Am7	D13	Gmaj7	

Am7	D11	Gmaj7
Am7♭5(Aø)	D7♭5 (also A♭7♭5)	Gm Gm+7 Gm7 Gm6
Am7♭5(Aø)	D7♭9	Gm

5th String roots	6th String roots	5th String roots
Dm	G	C
Dm7	G7	Cmaj7
Dm7	G7	Cmaj7 C6
Dm7sus	G7sus	C Csus C
Dm9	G13	Cmaj7
Dm7	G9	Cmaj7

Dm7	G7	Cadd9			
Dm7	G7	Cmaj9			
Dm7	G11	Cmaj7			
Dm7♭5(D∅)	G7♯5	Cm	Cm+7	Cm7	Cm6
Dm7	G7♭9	Cm7			

After you have practiced playing the columns from left to right as they are written, try playing any chord from the left column, change to any chord in the middle column, and then follow that chord with any chord from the right column. For example, change from Dm7 to G13 to C.

Chord Embellishment

Chord embellishment refers to "spicing up" the basic major and/or minor chords by adding more notes to make the chords richer and give them more color. For example, G7 has a more colorful sound than does a plain G chord. The information in this section of the book will show you what can be added to the basic chords in the key to make the chords sound more colorful. If you are playing by ear, this will help because you may have found the chord which sounds "almost correct" for a certain part of the song but is not quite right. By knowing what can be added to the chords, you can zero in on the exact chord to be used.

The first step in chord embellishment is to arrange all of the chords in a given key in alphabetical order. First, find the chords in a given key. **Use the chord clock** from the earlier section in this book to help you find all of the basic chords in a given key. For example, the chords in the key of C are C, F, G, Dm, Am and Em. Next, begin with the chord which has the same letter name as the key and arrange the chords in the key in alphabetical order. For example, the chords in the key of C arranged in alphabetical order would be C, Dm, Em, F, G and Am. Remember, in the musical alphabet A follows G. Practice arranging, in alphabetical order, the chords in the keys of G, D, A, E and F. Be sure to begin with the chord name which has the same letter name as the key. Next, once you have arranged the chords of the key in alphabetical order, assign each of the chords in the key a Roman numeral. The key chord (the chord which has the same letter name as the key) will be assigned the Roman numeral I. The second chord in the key (in alphabetical order) is the ii chord. The third chord in the key is iii, then IV, V, and vi. The following chart shows the chords in the key of D under the Roman numerals used to identify the chords.

I	ii	iii	IV	V	vi
D	Em	F♯m	G	A	Bm

The large Roman numerals are used on the I, IV and V chords because they are major chords. In every major key the I, IV and V chords are major. The small Roman numerals are used for the minor chords. In every major key ii, iii and vi chords are minor. Memorize the chords in the common keys of C, G, D, A, E and F. These are very popular keys for guitar. You could also figure out the six basic chords in each key by writing out the major scale of that key and then thinking of the Roman numeral order and which of the chords are major and which are minor. For example, if I wanted to find the chords in the key of A, I would write out the names of the notes in the A scale, which are: A, B, C♯, D, E, F♯ and G♯. Next, I would take the Roman numeral sequence (I, ii, iii, IV and vi) and match the notes of the A scale with the Roman numerals as shown on the chart below.

I	ii	iii	IV	V	vi	VII
A	B	C♯	D	E	F♯	G♯

Next, make the chords under the small Roman numerals minor.

I	ii	iii	IV	V	vi	VII
A	Bm	C♯m	D	E	F♯m	G♯dim

Notice that the VII chord is diminished. This chord does not appear on the chord clock. It is an uncommon chord to use in sing-along or campfire-type songs, but it would be good for you to know that it is in the key.

Now that you have assigned the basic chords in the key a Roman numeral, the chart below shows what embellishments can be added to the chords in the key. For example, in the key of C the IV chord is F. So, in the key of C you can play Fmaj7, F6, Fadd9, or any of the other embellishments for the IV chord. If you are playing a song in the key of C, and using the F chord sounds almost right in a certain place in the song, try playing the embellishments of the F chord until you find the correct one. Eventually, you should train your ear to hear the correct embellishment being used.

I, IV	major, sus, 6th, maj7, maj9, add9, 6/9, maj7♯11
V	major, 7, 7sus, 9, 11, 13, altered 7 (i.e. 7♯9, 7♭5)
ii	minor, m7, m7sus, m+7, m9 m6, m7♭5
iii, vi	minor, m7, m+7, m7sus m9

The following progression is in the key of D. The Roman numerals next to the chord names show what each chord is in the key. Every progression can be embellished hundreds of different ways. In jazz, every time you play a song you may use different embellishments. That's part of the beauty of playing jazz. You create it as you play it. After you practice playing the following progression, play it again, only this time add your own embellishments. Another good exercise is to play a folk song and embellish the chords. When you embellish a song or progression which is already written, first find what Roman numeral the chord is in the key, then by using the embellishment chart, "soup up" the chords.

 32

(82)

D(I)   G(IV)   D(I)   G(IV)   F♯m(iii)

Bm(vi)   Em(ii)   A(V)   D(I)

The next example shows some embellishment possibilities to the previous example. Your embellishment of the chord progression could be (and probably was) different than the one written below. The possible combinations of chord embellishments are vast.

 32

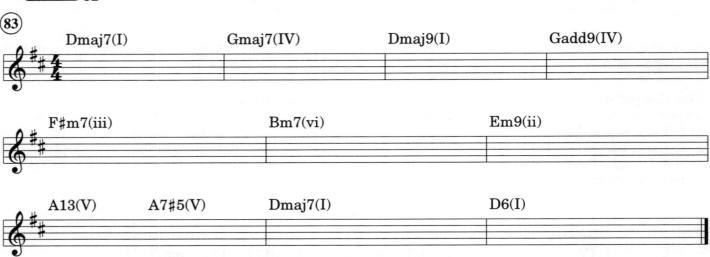

(83)

Dmaj7(I)   Gmaj7(IV)   Dmaj9(I)   Gadd9(IV)

F#m7(iii)   Bm7(vi)   Em9(ii)

A13(V)   A7#5(V)   Dmaj7(I)   D6(I)

To embellish a song in a minor key, the process is similar to that of a major key. For the purposes of this book, we will use the i, ii, iv and V chords in a minor key. The i chord in a minor key is a minor chord and is built upon the first step of the minor key. The i chord in A minor is Am. The ii chord in a minor key is built upon the second step of the minor scale and is a minor chord. Very often, the ii chord in a minor key will be a m7♭5 chord. For example, the ii chord in the key of A minor is Bm and usually Bm7♭5. The iv chord in a minor key is built upon the fourth step of the minor scale. It is also a minor chord. For example, the iv chord in the key of A minor is Dm. The V chord in a minor key is a major chord and usually a seventh chord. For example, the V chord in the key of A minor is E and usually E7.

The following chart shows how the chords in a minor key could be embellished.

i, iv	minor, m7, m+7, m9, m7sus
ii	minor, m7, m+7, m9, m7sus, m7♭5
V	major, 7, 7sus, 9, 11, 7♭9, 7#5, 7#5♭9

The next progression is in the key of Am. The Roman numerals showing what the chord is in relation to the key have been written in parentheses next to the chord names. Play the progression as written and then embellish the chords and play it again.

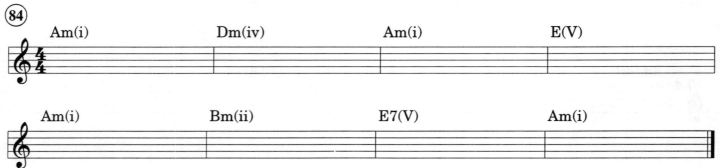

(84)

Am(i)   Dm(iv)   Am(i)   E(V)

Am(i)   Bm(ii)   E7(V)   Am(i)

The next progression shows one possibility of how the previous progression could be embellished.

(85)

Am7(i)	Dm7(iv)	Am7(i)	E7(V)

Am7(i)	Bm7♭5(ii)	E7♭5(V)	Am7(i)

How To Transpose

To *transpose* a song means to change the key. This may be necessary if the melody is too high or low for you to sing. Another reason for transposing a song could be that the chords may be too difficult for you to play. Transposing the song can make the chords easier. For example, if you have the music to a song which is in the key of B♭ and the chords to the song are B♭, E♭, Cm7 and F7, you could make the chords simpler by transposing the song into an easier key such as G. All of the chords to the song would then be made easier.

The chord clock can be used to transpose a song. To transpose a song, follow the steps written below.

1. Change the first chord in the piece to one of the simple key chords. Remember, the easiest keys for the guitar in order of difficulty are: G, C, D, A, E and F. The easiest minor keys are: Em, Am, Dm and Bm. You cannot change a major chord to a minor chord and vice versa. However, chords can be simplified. If you are transposing a chord name which sounds difficult to play, such as F13♭9, the chord names can be reduced. For example, a Dmaj7 can be reduced to a D chord, Em9 can be reduced to an Em chord, and a G13♭9 can be reduced to a G7 chord. To reduce chords, you can use the rules of embellishment in reverse. Basically, you are "unembellishing" the chords. Chords which have names larger than 7 can be reduced to 7 chords. The m9 chords can be reduced to m7 chords.

2. On the chord clock, find the original first chord of the song.

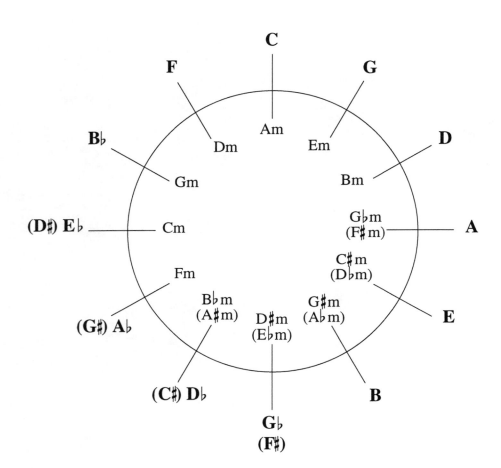

3. Find your new first chord on the chord clock. This is the new key in which you are playing.

4. See which direction (clockwise or counterclockwise) and how far (chord names) you moved on the chord clock to change the old original chord to the new chord.

5. Change the rest of the chords in the piece the same direction and distance on the chord clock as the first chord was changed. Major chords change to major chords and minor chords change to minor chords. If a chord in the song is not on the clock, reduce it to a chord name which does appear on the clock.

In the example below the clock, the original chord progression was in the key of B♭. The original chords are written on the bottom. The chords have been changed to the key of G. The new chords are written on the top. To change this progression from the key of B♭ to the key of G, the chords all had to be moved clockwise three steps or three moves on the chord clock as shown below. When transposing the Gm7 chord, a Gm was used. The Gm chord then moved to Em. If you want to use Em7 (putting the 7 back on), you can. Or, you can simply use Em. Notice that the F7♭5 has been changed to D7.

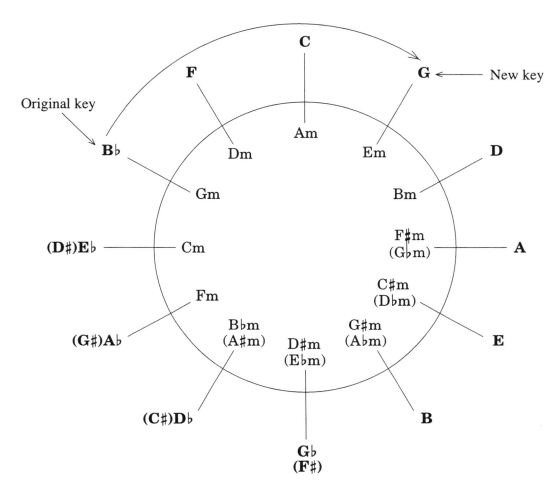

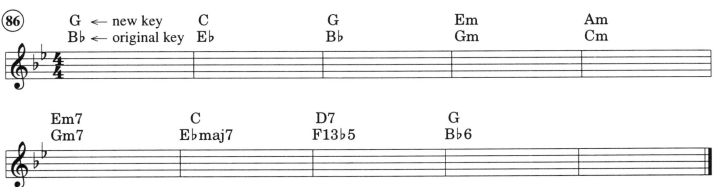

97

Transpose the following example from the key of E♭ to the key of C. In the case, the chords will be moving clockwise three steps, or three moves. Write the new chords above the old chord names.

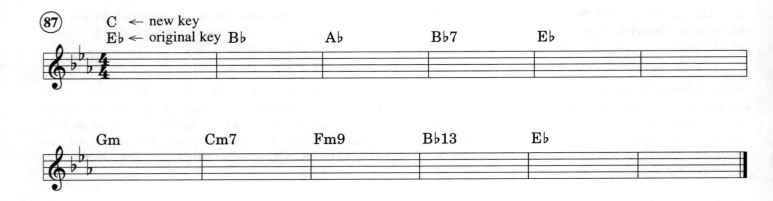

(87)   C   ← new key
        E♭ ← original key B♭   A♭   B♭7   E♭

        Gm   Cm7   Fm9   B♭13   E♭

Common Chord Progressions

Although any chord in the key can theoretically go to any other chord in the key, it is common for chords to progress in a certain order. For example, the most common progression in jazz is the ii-V-I chord progression. In the key of C this would be Dm to G to C. These chords could be embellished so the progression may be Dm7 to G7 to Cmaj7. The chart below shows some of the more common jazz chord progressions. Each progression should be practiced in many different keys and using several different fingerings. Written in parentheses, next to the Roman numerals, are what the chords would be in the key of C. It is important to transpose the progressions and play them in all keys. If you look at several different jazz standards, you will see just how popular these progressions are. Practice these progressions.

ii(Dm(7))—V(G(7))—I(C)

IV(F)—V(G(7))—I(C)

vi(Am(7))—ii(Dm(7))—V(G(7))—I(C)

iii(Em)—vi(Am)—ii(Dm)—V(G7)—I(C)

II(D7)—V(G7)—I(C)

vi(Am)—ii(Dm)—V(G7)—I(C)

vi(Am)—II(D7)—V(G7)—I(C)

VI(A7)—II(D7)—V(G7)—I(C)

iii(Em)—vi(Am)—ii(Dm)—V(G7)—I(C)

iii(Em)—vi(Am)—II(D7)—V(G7)—I(C)

iii(Em)—VI(A7)—II(D7)—V(G7)—I(C)

III(E7)—VI(A7)—II(D7)—V(G7)—I(C)

Practice playing all of the chord progressions written above. You should not only play these progressions in the key of C, but also transpose them and be able to play them in several keys.

Chord Substitution

The term *chord substitution* means the original chord has been replaced with a chord having another letter name (for example, replacing C9 with Gm7). Chord substitutions work because many of the notes in the chord which is being substituted are the same notes that are used in the original chord.

ii-V Substitution

One of the most common chord substitutions would be to substitute the ii chord for the V chord. In the key of C, you could substitute Dm (or Dm7) for G (or G7). This substitution can also work in reverse. The V chord can be substituted for the ii chord (i.e. G7 substitute for Dm).

The following example shows the ii-V substitution. The original chords are written on the bottom, and the substituted chords are written on the top.

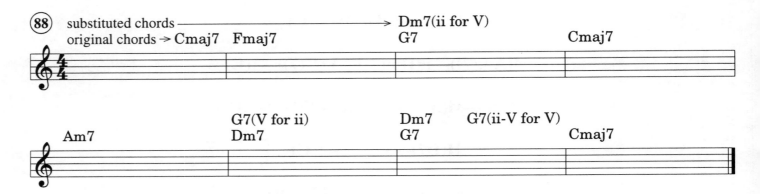

vi-I Substitution

Another common substitution is substituting the vi chord for a I chord. To do this, you have to imagine that any major chord in the progression is a I chord, even if it is not the I chord of the key in which you are playing. Then, substitute the relative minor (or the vi chord) of that major chord. As with all of the other chord substitutions, this can be done in reverse. To do this, imagine that whatever minor chord you are playing is a vi chord (even if it is not the vi chord in the key in which you are playing) and substitute its relative major (its I chord). The following example shows the vi-I chord substitution. The substituted chords are written in parentheses above the original chords. This substitution does not work on the V chord of the key in which you are playing. For example, in the key of C, this substitution will not work on the G chord.

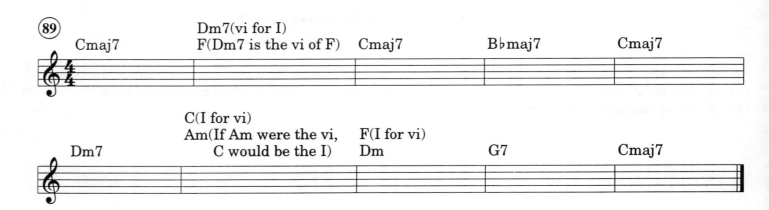

100

iii-I Substitution

Another substitution is done by substituting the iii chord for the I chord. In this case, if a major chord is played, imagine it is the I chord (even if it's not) and substitute what would be its iii chord. If a minor chord is played, imagine it is the iii chord and substitute what would be its I chord. The following progression shows this substitution.

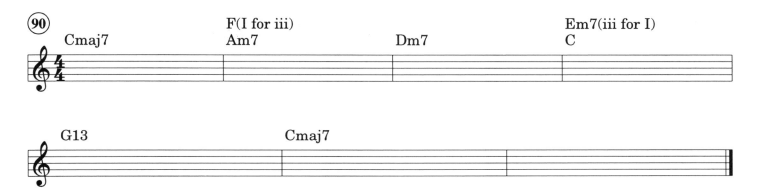

In the following song, the vi-I, and iii-I substitutions have been used. Notice how much more harmonically colorful the song becomes with the addition of the new substituted chords.

Shenandoah

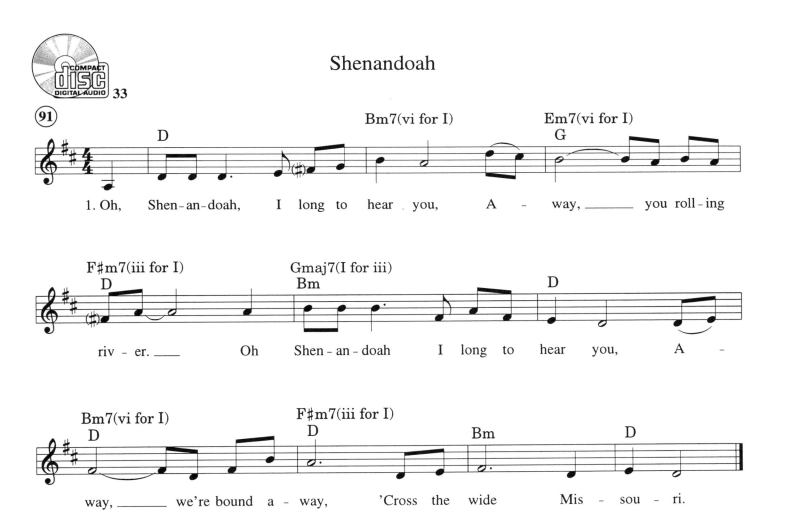

101

♭V of V Substitution

A good substitution for the V chord in the key is to use the ♭V of V. This is sometimes called the tritone substitution. For example, if you are playing in the key of C and a G7 chord is played, you could substitute D♭7 for G7 because D♭ is the ♭V of G. Very often the ♭V chord will be a 7♭5. This is popular because the 7♭5 of the substituted chord contains three of the same notes as the original chord (hence the term *tritone*). The next progression shows the use of the ♭V of V.

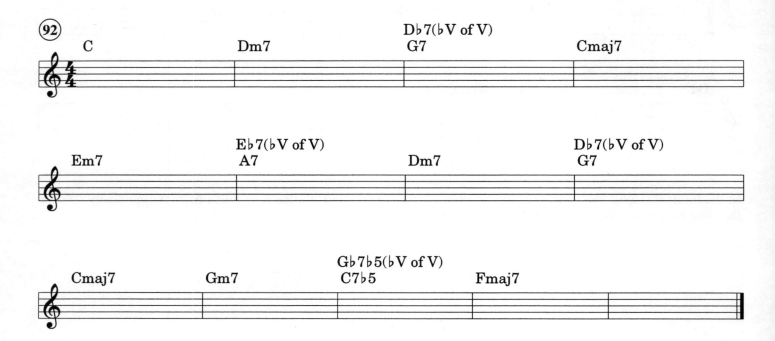

Backcycling

Backcycling is a type of chord substitution which is commonly used in jazz, especially in the last one or two measures of a piece if the music is going to be repeated. This part of the music is commonly called the *turnaround*. To backcycle, precede any chord in the progression with its ii-V chords. The original chords (whatever they may be) can be omitted to use the ii-V. The next example shows the F chord being preceded with its ii-V (Gm7 and C7).

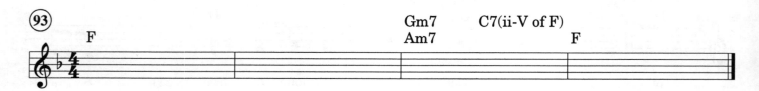

You can continue the backcycling process for as long as you like, by preceding the new ii-V with the ii-V of the ii chord. The next example shows how this done.

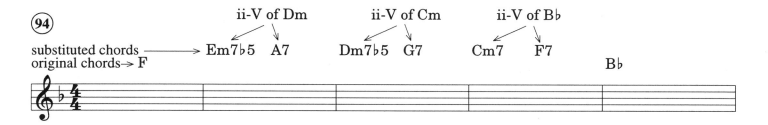

This type of substitution is called *backcycling* because you do it going backwards.

The following progression contains backcycling substitutions.

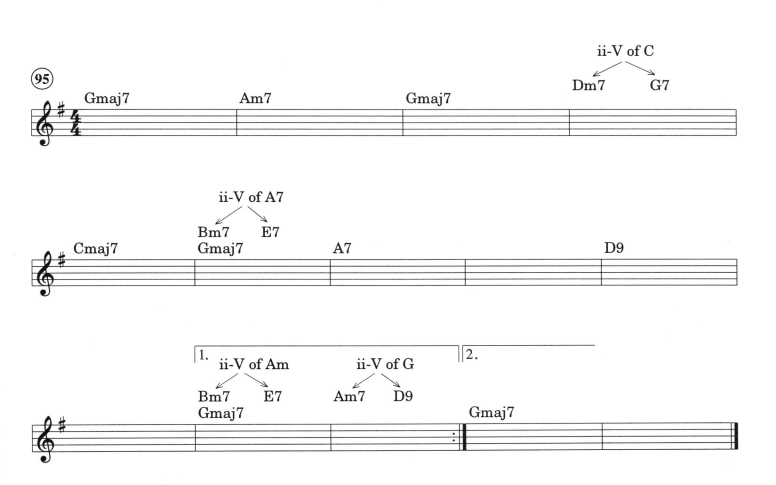

The next progression is a blues in the key of C. Backcycling has been used in the last two measures to create a turnaround before the progression is repeated.

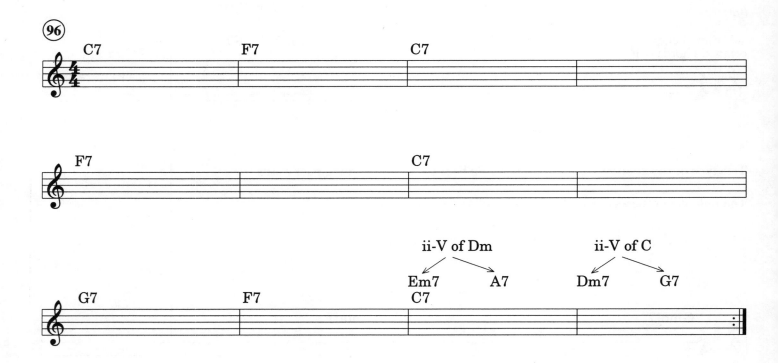

Diatonic Substitution

Diatonic substitution is another form of chord substitution. In using this type of substitution, chords are connected, or a progression is "filled in," with chords from the key moving in alphabetical order. In the next progression, the Cmaj7 chord is connected to the Fmaj7 chord with Dm7 and Em7. This works because Dm7 and Em7 are the two chords in the key that connect C to F alphabetically.

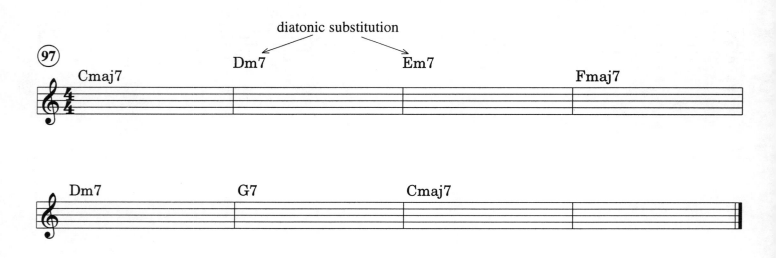

In the following example, the original progression had a place where the Amaj7 was held for a long time. To add interest, chords from the key of A were added going up and down alphabetically.

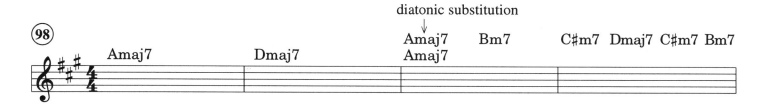

The chart below shows the various chord substitutions. The chords on the left are the original chords and the chords on the right may be substituted for them. Roman numerals have been used so that these substitutions can be made in any key. The chord names in parentheses show what the chords would be in the key of C.

ii(Dm) ⟷ V(G)
I(C) ⟷ vi(Am)
I(C) ⟷ iii (Em)
♭V(D♭7) ⟷ V(G7)

Backcycling - precede any chord with its ii-V.
Diatonic - play chords from the key in alphabetical order, or connect two chords alphabetically with chords from the key.

The following progression is in the key of B♭. The original chords are on the bottom and the substituted chords are written above them. As you can see, many different substitutions can be used. Practice playing the following progression several times.

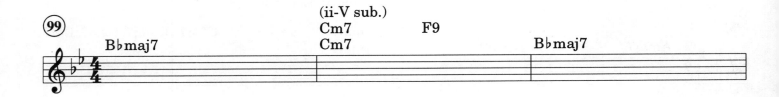

(99)

	(ii-V sub.)		
	Cm7	F9	
B♭maj7	Cm7		B♭maj7

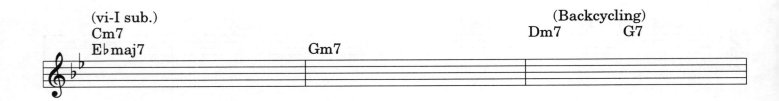

(vi-I sub.)		(Backcycling)	
Cm7		Dm7	G7
E♭maj7	Gm7		

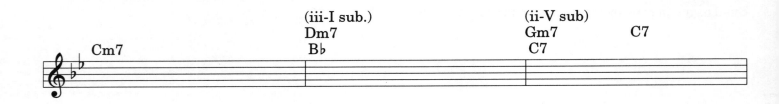

	(iii-I sub.)	(ii-V sub)	
	Dm7	Gm7	C7
Cm7	B♭	C7	

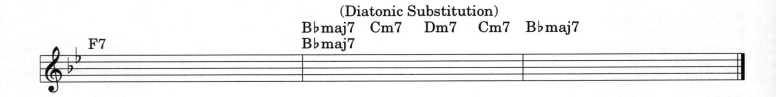

	(Diatonic Substitution)
	B♭maj7 Cm7 Dm7 Cm7 B♭maj7
F7	B♭maj7

The following arrangement of *Silent Night* contains several embellishments and chord substitutions. The substitutions have been labeled. Notice how a tune like *Silent Night* can be transformed into a jazz arrangement by using chord substitution.

Silent Night

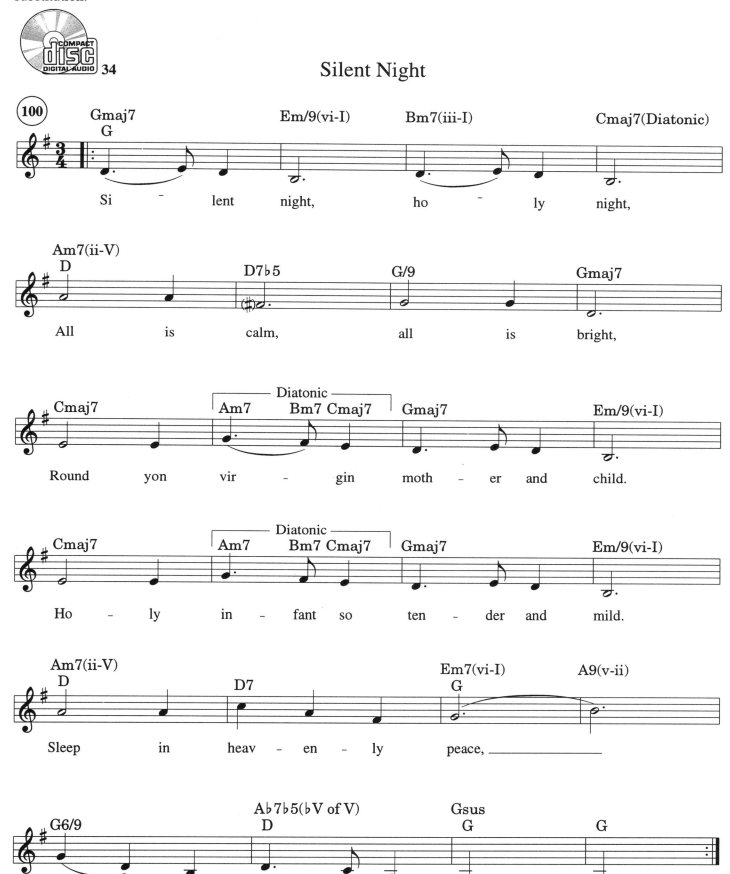

Written below is a basic chord progression in the key of G. Places where chord substitutions could occur have been labeled. Change the progression using chord substitutions. Write the new substituted chords above the original ones.

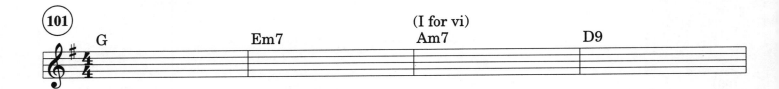

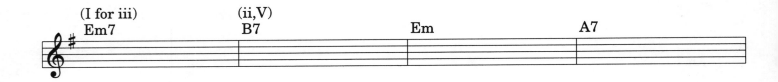

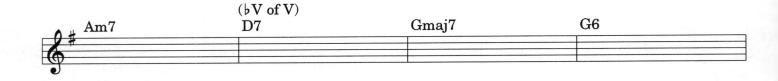

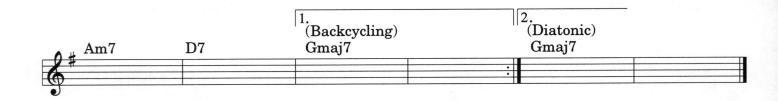

Depending on how "outside" you want the sound to be, it is possible to do a substitution of a substitution. For example, one could backcycle to C by playing Dm7 to G7 to C. Then use the ♭V substitution by playing D♭7 in place of the G7.

The following progression started out being F to C and ended up being F-Dm7-D♭7-C.

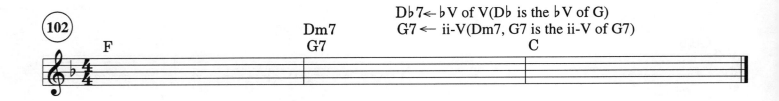

The following examples show progressions where a chord substitution has been made on top of another substitution. The original chords are written on the bottom. The first chord substitutions are written above the original chords. Finally, the second substituted chords (the substitutions of the substitutions) are written on the top.

Fmaj.7 ←— I for iii (F is the I if Am is the iii)
Am7 ←— vi for I (Am is the vi of C)

(103)

C Dm7 G7 Cmaj7

Dm7 Db7 ←— bV of V (Db is the bV of G)
Dm7 G7 ←— ii-V (Dm7 is the ii if G is the V)

E7 Dm7 G7 Cmaj7

Em7 Eb7 ←— bV of V
Em7 A7 ←— ii-V
A7 Dm7 G7 Cmaj7

109

Blues Progression

Blues is an essential element in learning to play jazz guitar. Many jazz standards are written to blues progressions. It's important that you memorize the basic blues progression and its variations. The first type of blues you should learn is the standard 12-bar blues progression. This format is 12 measures long and in its basic form, uses only three chords. So you can play the blues in any key, learning the formula for the progression using Roman numerals. The chords used in the basic blues are the I, IV, and V chords. The Roman numeral "I" represents the key. The I chord will have the same letter names as the key in which you are playing. For example, the I chord in the key of C is C. The IV chord is four steps up the major scale from the I chord. The IV chord in the key of C is F. The V chord is five steps up the major scale from the I chord. The V chord in the key of C is G. The chart below shows the I, IV, and V chords in the various keys.

Key

I	IV	V
A	D	E
Bb	Eb	F
B	E	F#
C	F	G
C#	F#	G#
D	G	A
Eb	Ab	Bb
F	Bb	C
F#	B	C#
G	C	D
Ab	Db	Eb

The formula for the basic 12-bar blues progression is four measures of the I chord, two measures of the IV chord, two measures of the I chord, one measure of the V chord, one measure of the IV chord, and two measures of the I chord. The next example is the basic blues progression in the key of C. Seventh chords are commonly used on every chord in the blues progression, not for any theoretical reason, but because they sound dissonant and have that "times are tough" sound. Strum down four times in a measure, or use comp patterns on these exercises.

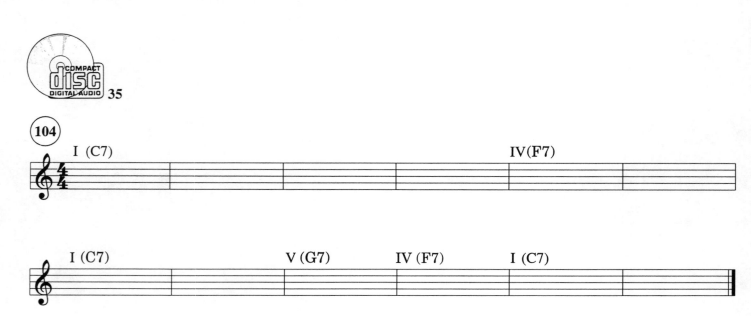

A common variation on the blues progression is to play the IV chord in the second measure. The next progression contains this chord.

105

I(C7)　　　IV(F7)　　　I(C7)　　　　　　　　IV(F7)

I(C7)　　　　　　　V(G7)　　IV(F7)　　I(C7)

It's also common to play the V chord in the last measure if the progression is gong to be repeated.

36

106

I(C7)　　　IV (F7)　　　I(C7)　　　　　　　IV(F7)

I(C7)　　　　　　　V(G7)　　IV(F7)　　I (C7)　　V (G7)

It is a very common practice to use chord embellishment when playing the blues. In the next example, the original chords are written on the bottom and the top chords are the embellished and/or substituted chords.

107
A7　　A9　　D9　　　　A7　　Bb7　A13　　　D9　　　　D13　　D9
A7　　　　　D7　　　　A7　　　　　A7　　　　D7　　　　D7

A7　　　A7#9　　E9　　　　D9　　　　A7　　　　E7#9
A7　　　A7　　　E7　　　　D7　　　　A7　　　　E7

111

The last two measures of the blues progression are often referred to as the *turnaround*. This refers to last two measures "setting up" the repeat of the progression. Backcycling substitution is often used for the turnaround. The next progression in the key of C shows the turnaround in the last two measures.

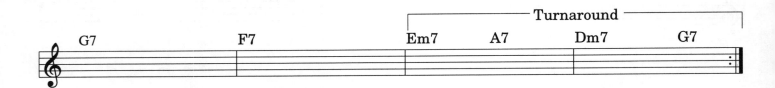

The next two progressions show other common variations on the blues progression. Notice the use of chord embellishments and chord substitutions. Pratice these progressions as written and then transpose them into other keys.

 37

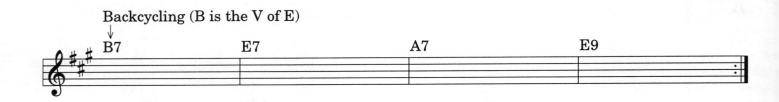

112

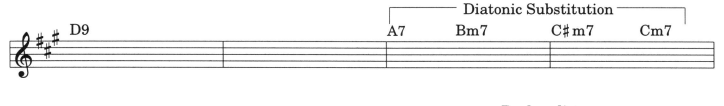

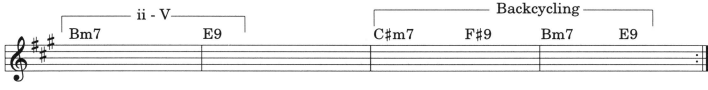

In a minor key, the formula for the blues is the same as for a major key, except the i and iv chords are minor. The V chord is still a major (and usually a seventh chord or some other chord from the dominant seventh family). The following progression shows a minor blues in the key of Am.

The next blues progression shows a variation on the twelve bar minor blues in the key of Am.

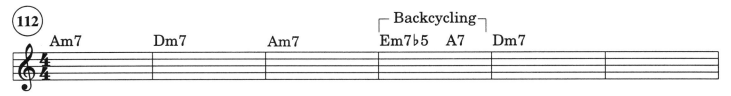

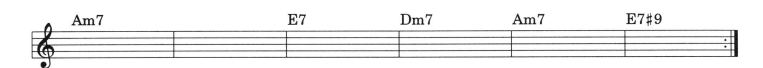

Pentatonic Scales

A pentatonic scale is a five-note scale. We will be working with two types of pentatonic scales, minor and major. The minor pentatonic scale is a natural minor scale with the half steps omitted. This is a very popular scale. It can be used to improvise to minor chords and seventh-type chords (7th, 9th, 13, etc.), and it's also a very popular scale to use when improvising to the blues. The notes of an A minor pentatonic scale are written below.

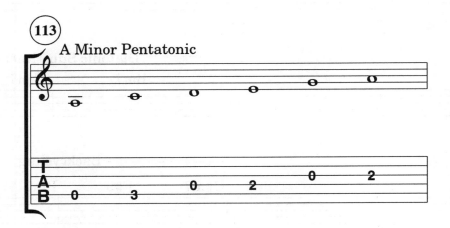

Some common moveable fingerings for the minor pentatonic scale are drawn below. The diamonds indicate the location of the roots. One has the root on the sixth string, and the other has the root on the fifth string. Practice these scales.

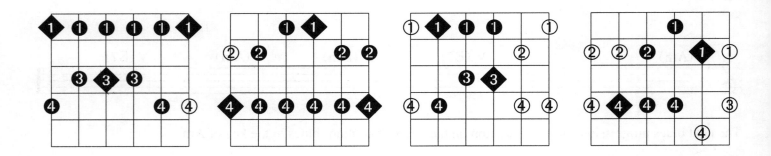

114

The following two solos use the minor pentatonic scale. The first solo is to a blues progression in the key of A minor, and the second is a blues in C. The first solo uses the A minor pentatonic scale with the root on the sixth string, fifth fret. The second solo uses the C minor pentatonic scale with the root on the fifth string, third fret.

The diagrams below show extensions of the minor pentatonic scale. The circled areas show the extensions of the original minor pentatonic scale.

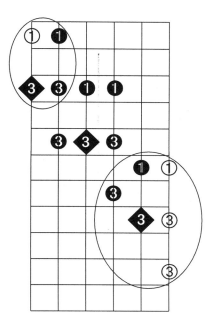
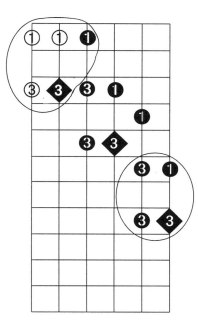

The major pentatonic scale is a major scale with the half steps missing. The notes in a C major pentatonic scale are shown below.

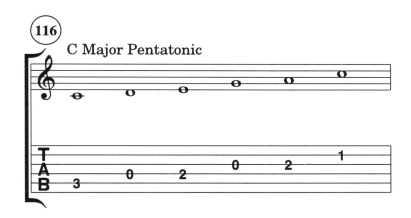

Patterns for the moveable major pentatonic scale are given below. Some have the root on the sixth string, and the others have the root on the fifth string. Again, the black diamonds indicate the location of the roots. Practice these patterns.

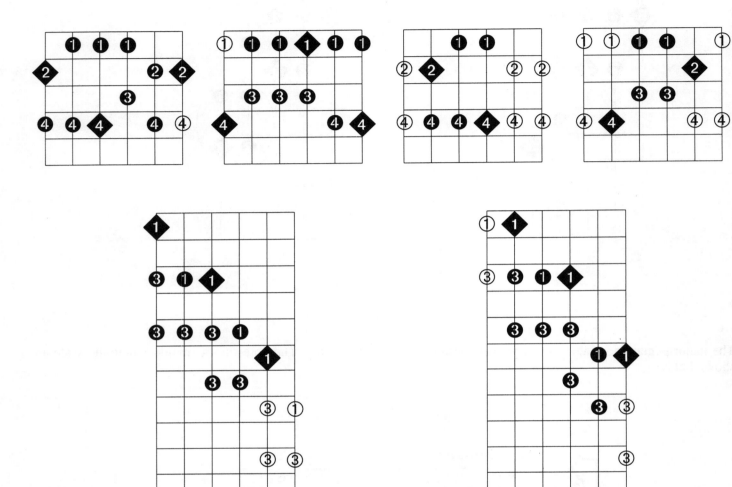

The major pentatonic scale can be used to improvise over any progression which uses chords from the major key. For example, use C major pentatonic to improvise to any chord in the key of C (C, Dm, Em, F, G, Am). If the key changes, you must change the scale. Like the minor pentatonic scale, it can also be used to improvise over a blues progression.

The following solo uses the major pentatonic scale. The solo is over chords in the key of D and uses the D major pentatonic scale with the root on the fifth string, fifth fret. Even if the chords change, as long as they are from the same key, the scale which has the name of the key can be used to solo for the entire progression. After you can play the written solo, improvise your own solos to these same chord changes using the D major pentatonic scale.

Blues Scale

The blues scale contains the same notes as the minor pentatonic scale plus the addition of a flatted fifth. The blues scale is built with the following: root, flat third, fourth, flat fifth, natural fifth, and flat seventh. The notes in the C blues scale are shown below.

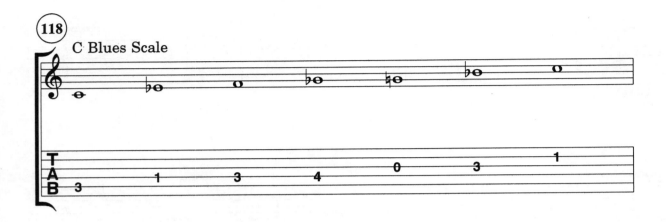

Drawn on the diagrams below are two of the most common moveable fingerings for the blues scale. The pattern on the left has the root on the sixth string and the pattern on the right has the root on the fifth string. Memorize these patterns.

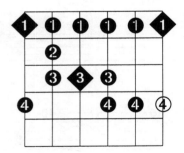

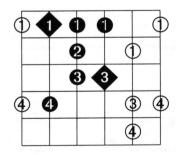

The diagrams below show extensions of the blues scale. The circled areas show the extensions.

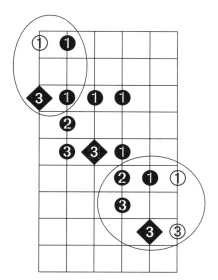 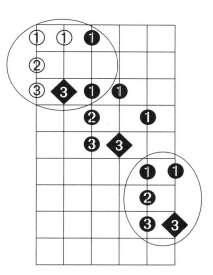

The blues scale can be used to improvise over seventh chords and other chords from the dominant seventh chord family (i.e. 9, 11, 13, 7#9, etc.). If the blues scale is being used to improvise to the blues progression, you can play the blues scale which has the same letter name as the key in which you are playing. As the chords to the progression change, you don't have to change scale. You can continue to play the scale which has the same letter name as the key. The following solo shows the A blues scale being used for a solo to the blues in the key of A. When the chords of the progression change, the A blues scale is still used. The blues scale which is used in this solo has the root on the sixth string, fifth fret (A).

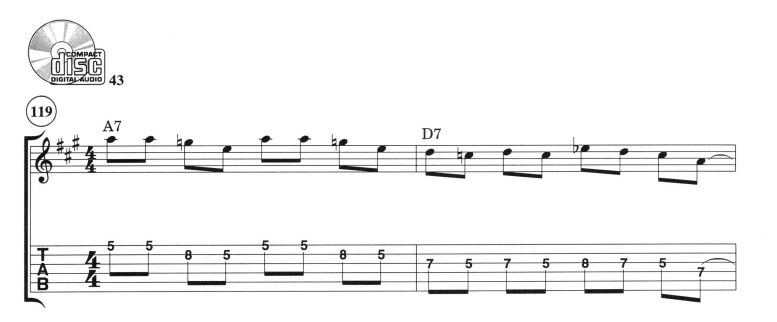

121

122

The blues scale can also be used to play over minor chords and other chords from the minor family (i.e. m7, m9, etc.). In the next solo, the Dm blues scale with the root on the fifth string, fifth fret (D) is used over the minor blues progression in the key of Dm. Again, when the chords in the progression change, the scale which is used doesn't.

Sequencing

A *sequence* is when a pattern of notes is repeated with the first note of the pattern ascending or descending through a scale or arpeggio. For example, a sequence pattern may consist of going three notes up the major scale and then returning to the beginning note like this:

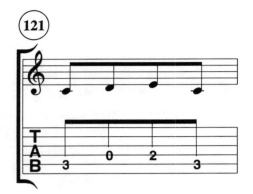

The sequence can begin on any note in the scale. After the pattern has been established, it is repeated with the first note of the pattern ascending or descending a scale like this:

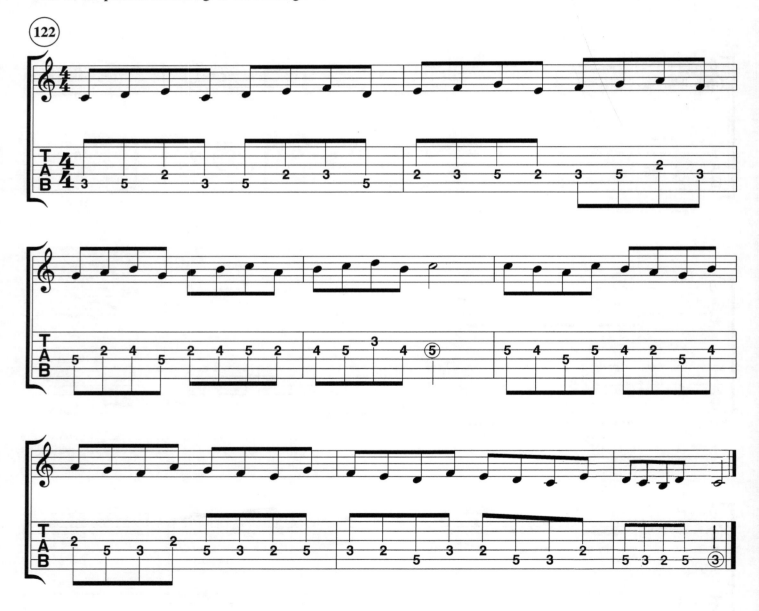

Written below are several common sequence patterns using the major scale. Practice each of them and then try creating some of your own sequences. The beginning of each sequence is written. Continue each sequence pattern through (or beyond) an octave. Be sure to practice the sequences ascending and descending using several major scale patterns. Also, practice these sequences using the other moveable major scale patterns.

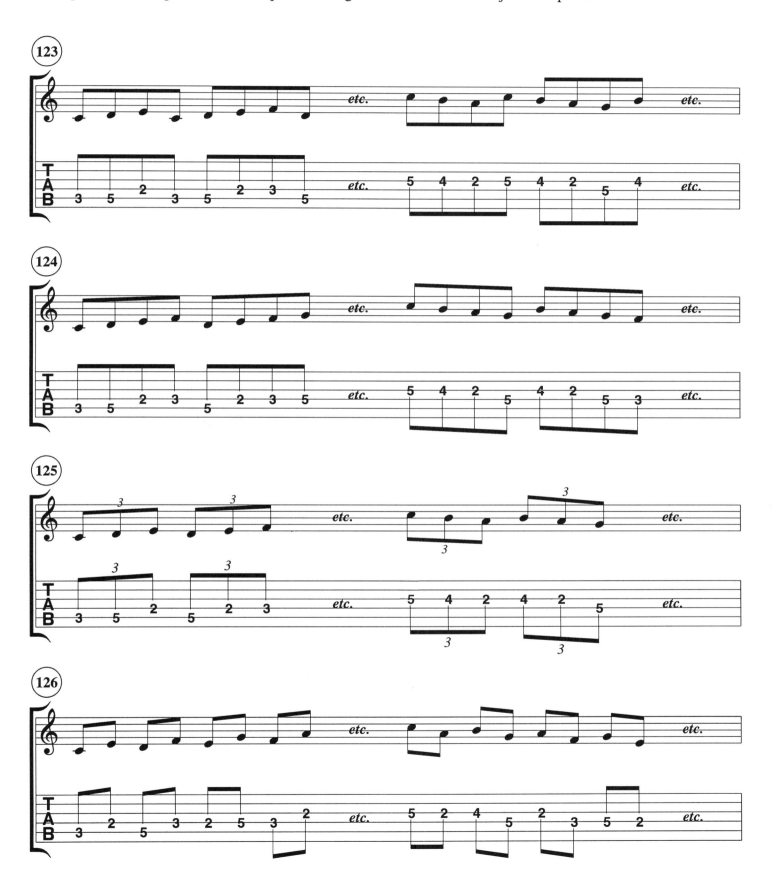

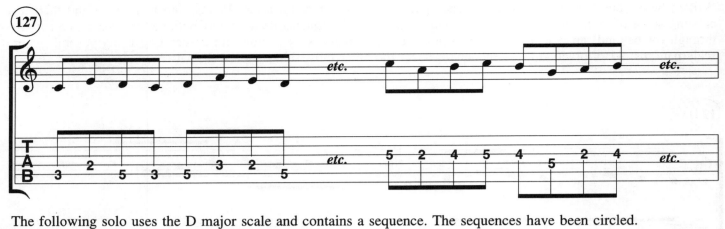

The following solo uses the D major scale and contains a sequence. The sequences have been circled.

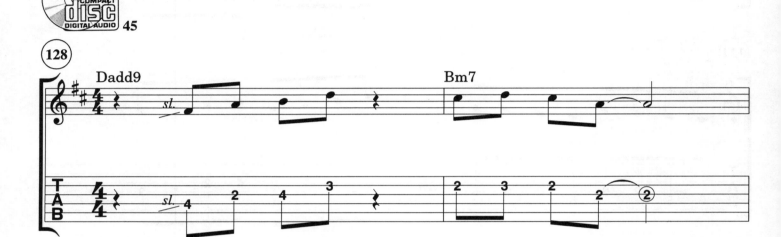

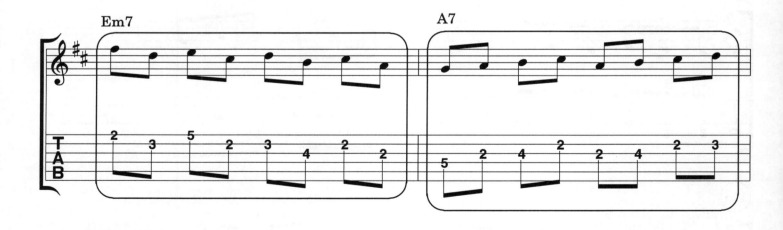

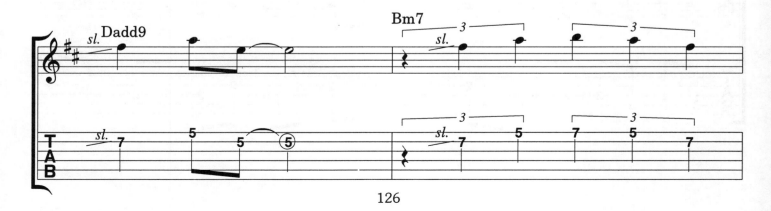

126

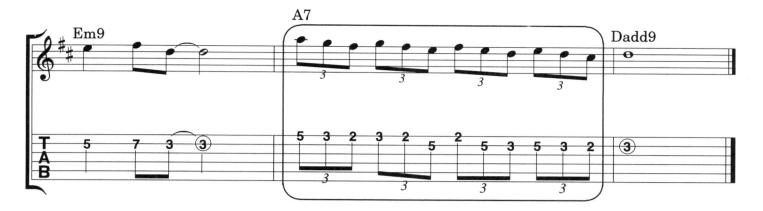

The sequences written below use the A harmonic minor scale.

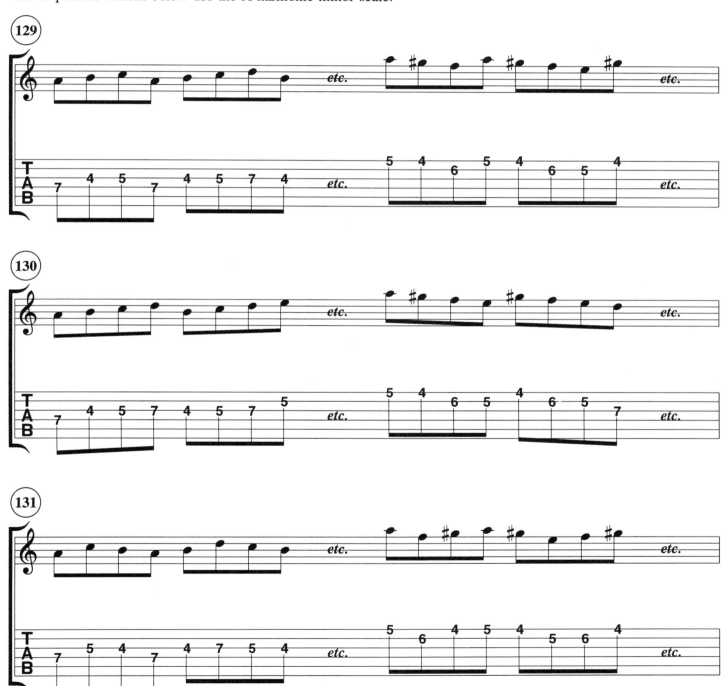

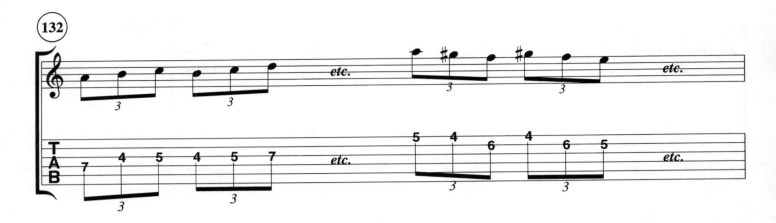

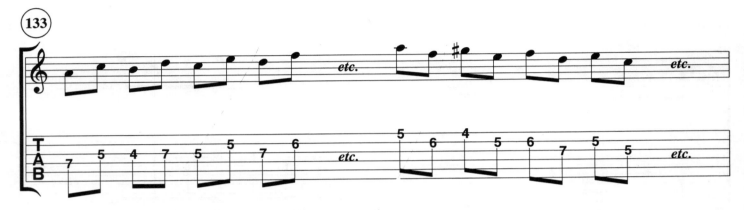

The next solo uses the A harmonic minor scale and contains a sequence.

 46

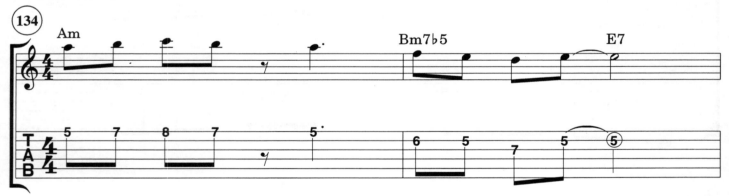

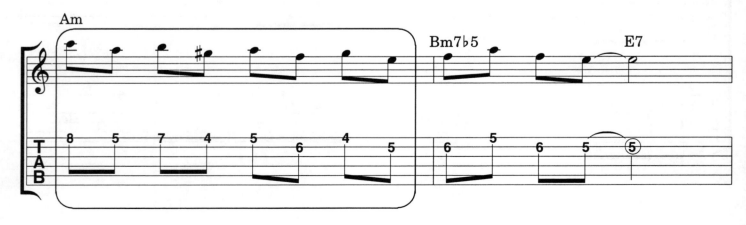

The following sequences use the A minor pentatonic scale. Practice these patterns.

129

The following solo contains sequences using the A minor pentatonic scale.

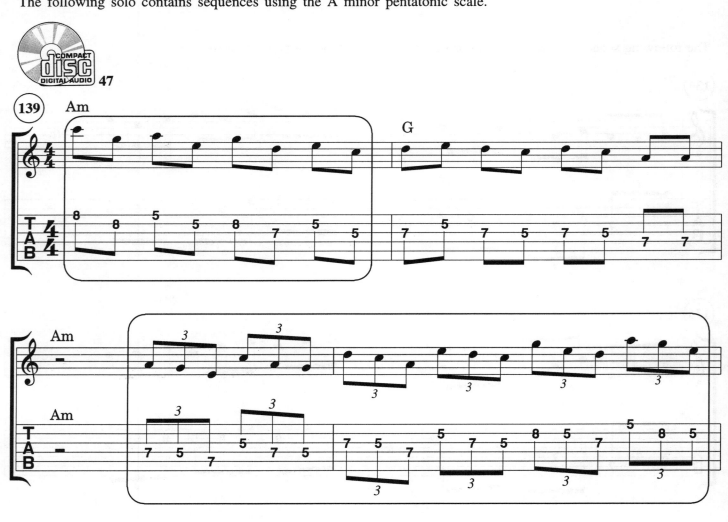

The following solo contains sequences using the C major pentatonic scale.

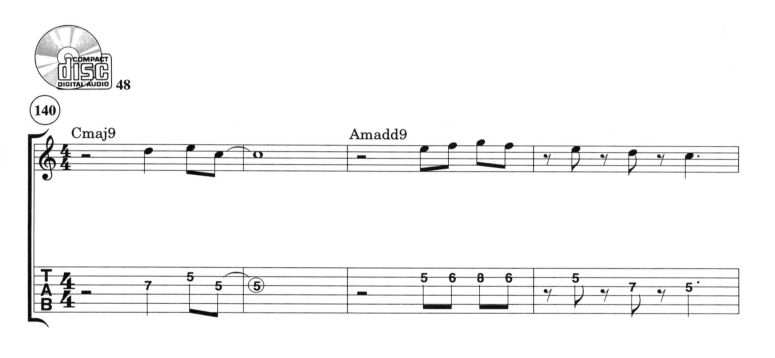

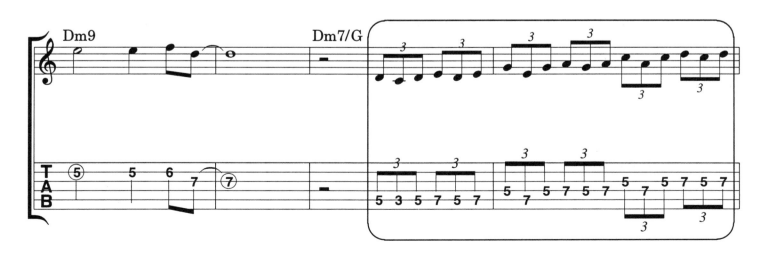

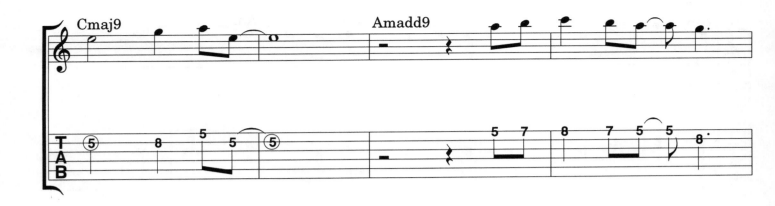

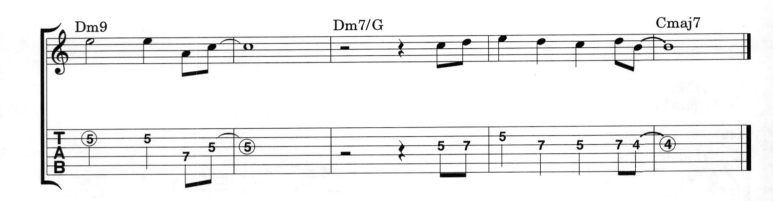

Diminished Chords

The diminished chord (sometimes called the diminished seventh chord) is written as, dim or with a small circle next to the chord name. The diminished chord is built with a series of three minor thirds. Drawn below are the three most common fingerings for the diminished chords. These patterns are moveable just like the barre chords and dead string chords. The diminished chord is unique in that each note in the chord can be the root of the chord. For that reason, it is called *symmetrical*. Each diminished chord fingering is actually four chords in one. Although each note in the chord can be the root, the diminished chords are often positioned and voiced so the lowest note which is played is considered to be the root of the chord. On the patterns below, one pattern has the root on the sixth string, one has the root on the fifth string, and one has the root on the fourth string.

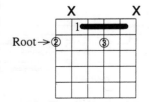

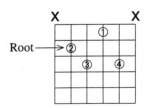

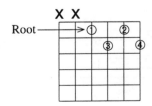

The diminished chord is often used to connect chords which are a whole step apart. For example, Am7 could be connected to Bm7 with an A#dim chord. Practice playing the following progressions which contain diminished chords. Play the patterns which are drawn next to the chord names.

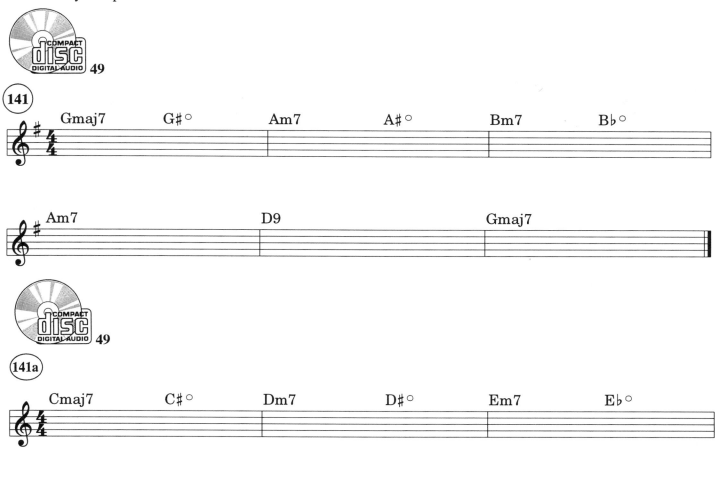

Diminished Scale

The diminished scale is sometimes called the whole-half scale, or the half-whole scale. It is based on a series of alternating whole and half steps. If the diminished scale begins with a whole step (whole step, half step, whole step, half step, etc.), then this scale can be used to improvise or create melodies for diminished chords which have the same letter name as the scale (i.e., play a C diminished scale over a C diminished chord). Drawn below are the notes of the C diminished scale beginning with a whole step.

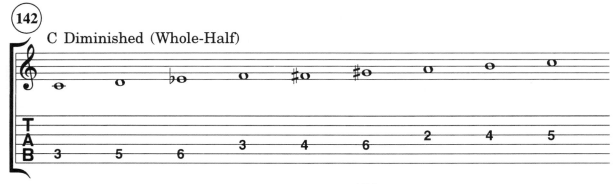

133

The diagrams below show some common fingerings for the diminished scale beginning with whole step.

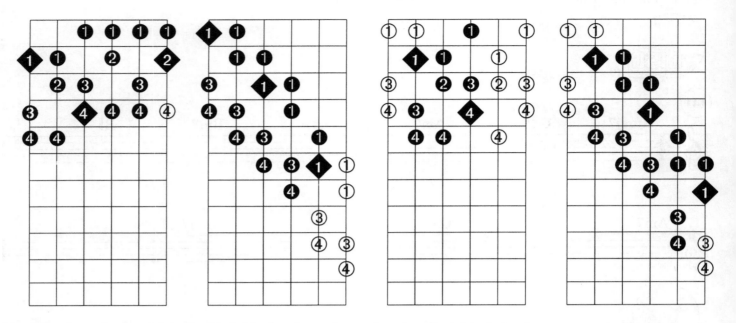

The following solo shows how the diminished scale can be used against diminished chords.

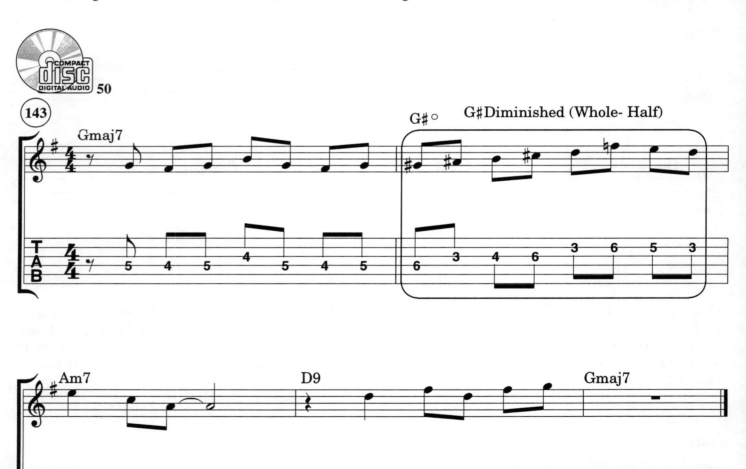

If the diminished scale begins with a half step (half step, whole step, half step, whole step, etc.), then this scale can be used to improvise or write melodies to 7♭9 chords. For example, use a G diminished scale beginning with a half step to improvise over a G7♭9 chord.

Written below is the C diminished scale beginning with a half step.

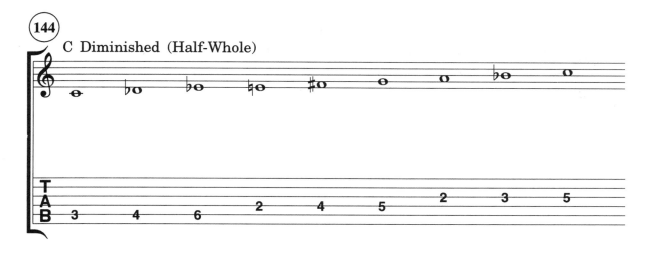

The following diagrams show some common fingerings for the diminished scale beginning with a half step.

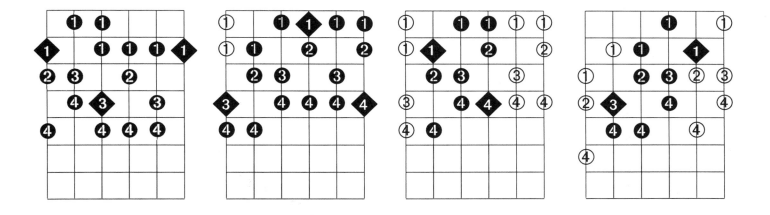

135

Practice the following solo which uses the diminished scale against the 7♭9 chords.

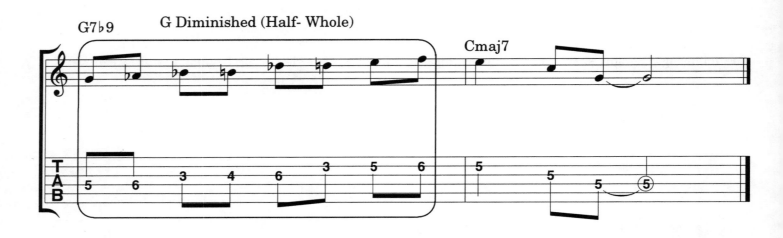

Augmented Chords

Augmented chords are written with aug or a small plus sign (+) next to the chord letter name. They are built with two major third intervals. Like the diminished chord, each note in the augmented chord can be the root. Also, like the diminished chord, the augmented chord pattern is usually positioned so the lowest note played is considered to be the root. Drawn below are three of the more common fingerings for the augmented chord.

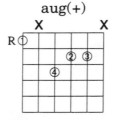

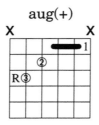

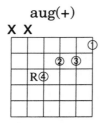

Practice the following progressions which contain augmented chords.

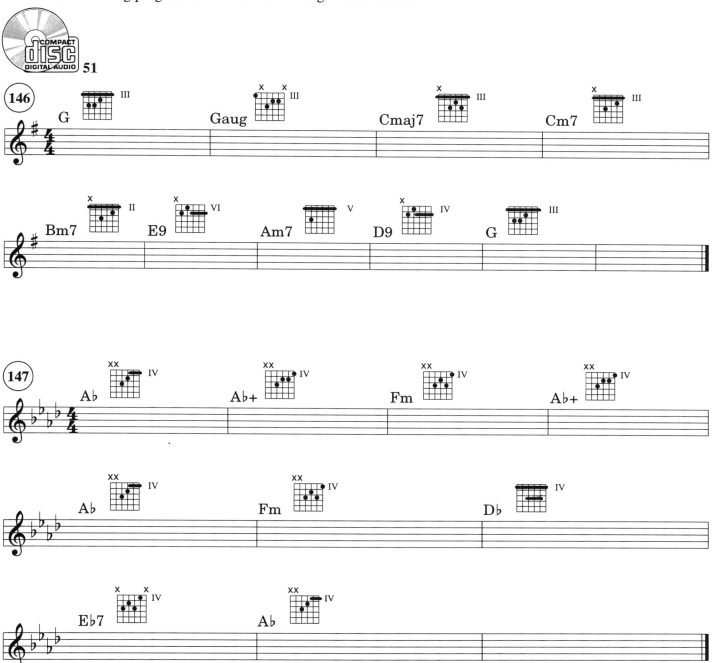

The augmented chord is often used to connect notes from two different chords. The notes to be connected are a whole step apart. For example, Faug could be used to connect an F chord to a B♭ chord (F-Faug-B♭), because the C note in the F chord is being connected to the D note in the B♭ chord by using the C♯ note from the Faug chord.

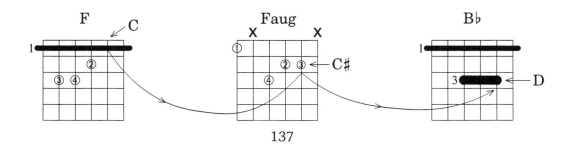

Whole Tone Scale

The whole tone scale is built on a series of whole steps. This scale has seven notes in one octave. The notes for a C whole tone scale are shown below. Because after every whole step the notes will be the same, there are only two whole tone scales (i.e. C whole tone = D whole tone).

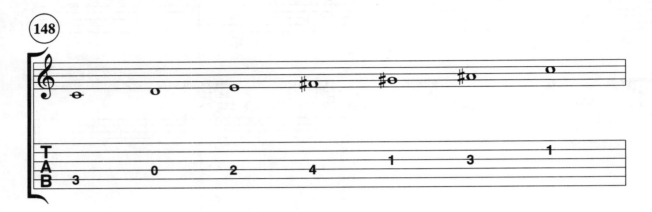

Drawn on the diagrams below are six fingerings for the whole tone scale.

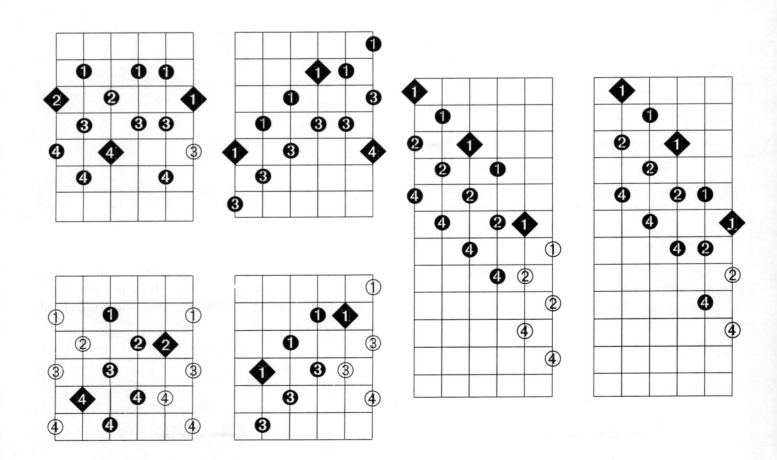

The notes of this scale can be used to improvise over augmented and seventh chords in which the fifth has been altered (i.e. 7♭5, 7♯5, etc.). The following solos show how the whole tone scale can be used to improvise over these chords.

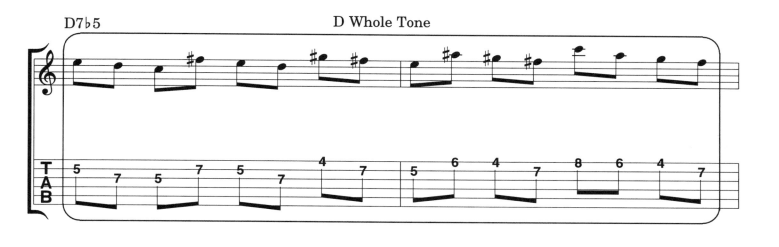

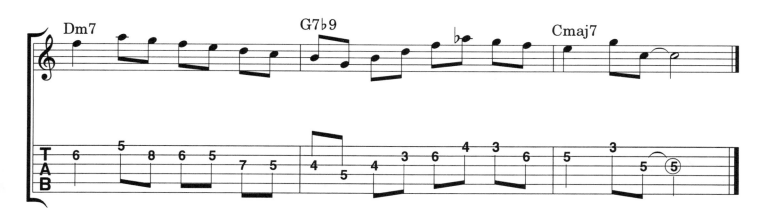

Latin Rhythms

The use of Latin rhythms is another ingredient which is common in jazz guitar. Written below are many Latin-style accompaniment patterns. Above each pattern is written the name of the dance style which is associated with that rhythm. These patterns can be used to accompany many songs in 4/4. The "laid-back" feeling that they create makes them fun to play and listen to. If you are improvising to these rhythms, be sure to use straight eighth notes rather than swing-style playing.

Hold any chord and practice each rhythm.

The "P" that is written represents the picking of the bass string of the chord which is being held. For example, with G7, the sixth string is picked. In the first two Bossa Nova patterns, the strum is done by pulling strings rather than strumming across them. The strings which are pulled are either strings 1, 2, and 3 or 2, 3, and 4. These strings are pulled with right-hand fingers 1, 2, and 3.

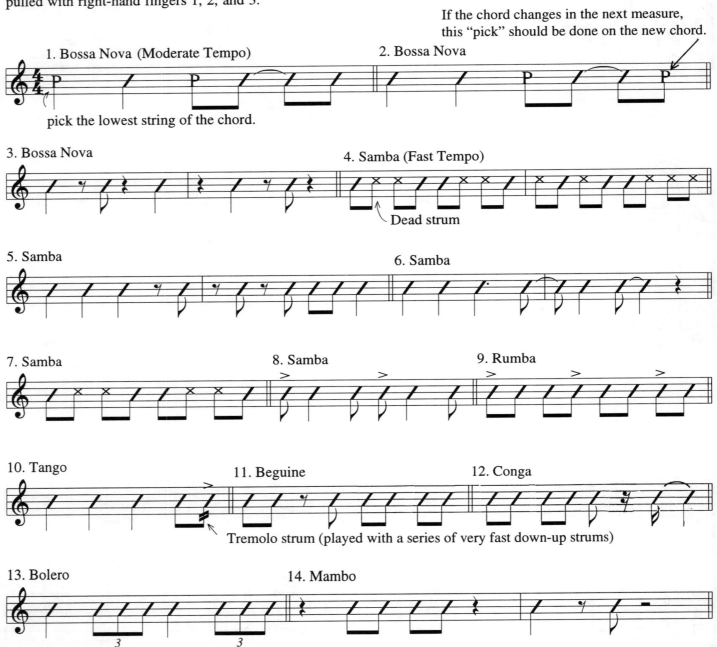

Practice the following progressions. In each measure, use the pattern which is written in the first measure.

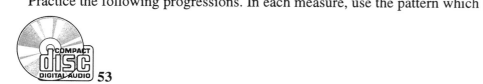

53

(150) ─ pattern #1 (Bossa Nova)

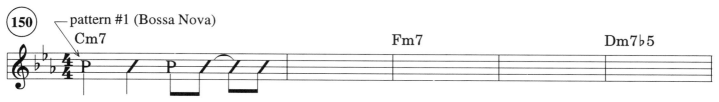

54

(151) ─ pattern #2 (Bossa Nova)

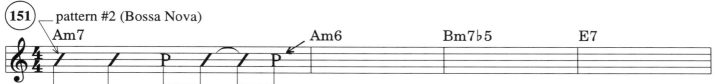

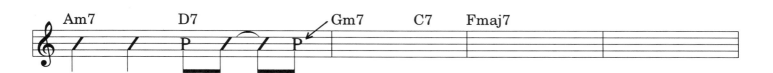

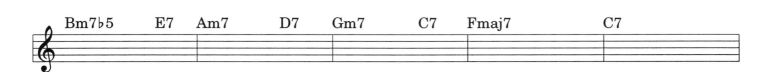

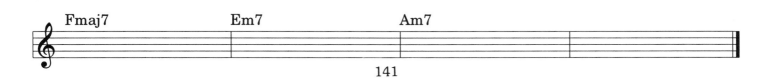

Dorian Mode

The Dorian mode is a major scale beginning on the second degree. For example, if you play the notes of a C major scale and you start on the second note of the scale (D), you will be playing the D Dorian mode. To play E Dorian, play the notes of a D major scale, only start on the second step of the scale (E). The letter name of the Dorian mode you want to play will have the same notes as the major scale which is one whole step lower (i.e., G Dorian = F major).

The notes of the D Dorian mode are shown below.

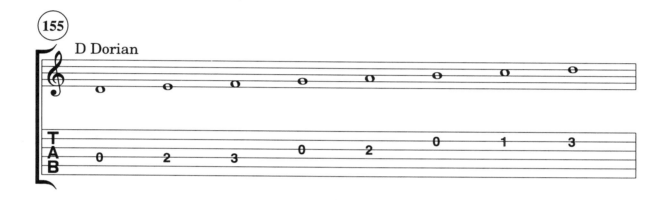

The most popular moveable fingerings for the Dorian mode are drawn on the diagrams below.

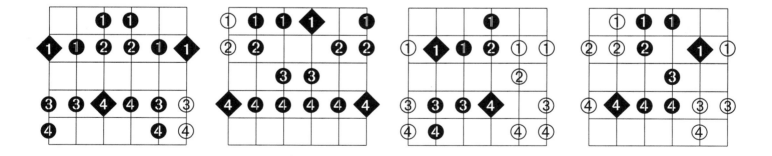

The Dorian mode can be used to improvise over minor chords and other chords from the minor family. For example, for Cm7 use C Dorian.

The following solo uses the D Dorian mode over a Dm7 chord and E♭ Dorian over the E♭m7 chord.

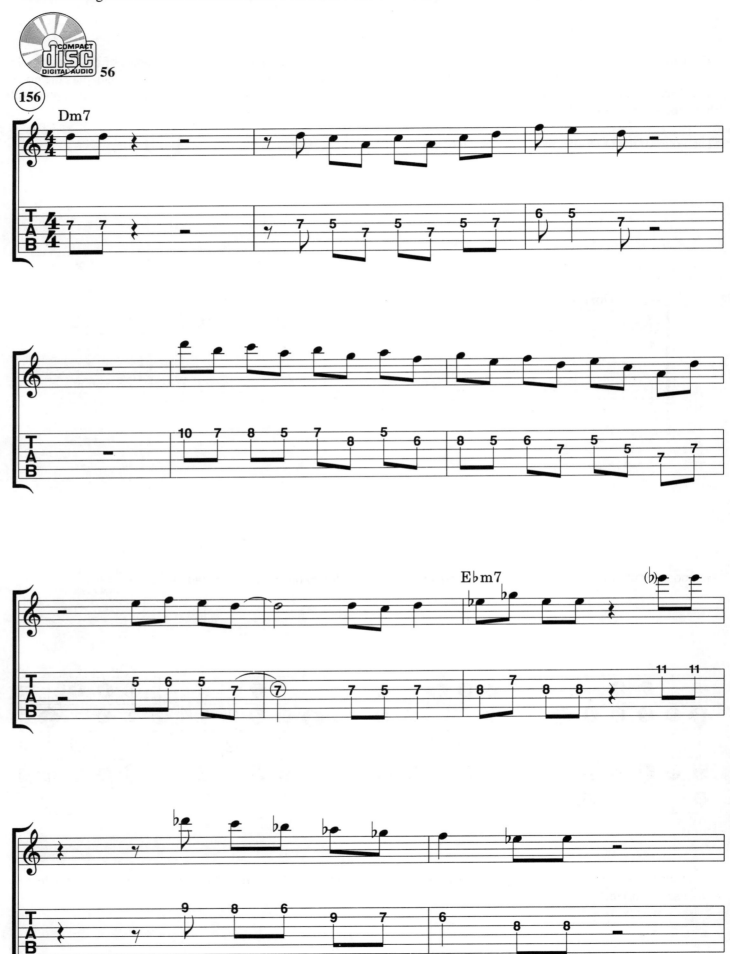

The Dorian mode can also be used to improvise to a chord progression which consists of a minor chord going to a major chord which is a fourth away. The following solo shows how this is done. The chords are Am to D and the solo uses notes in the A Dorian mode.

Another place the Dorian mode can be used is when the chord progression has a minor chord going to another minor chord which is a whole step higher. The next solo shows how the Dorian mode is used this way. The chords are Cm7 to Dm7. The C Dorian mode is used for the solo.

Mixolydian Mode

The Mixolydian mode is a major scale with a flat seventh degree. The notes in the C Mixolydian mode are shown below.

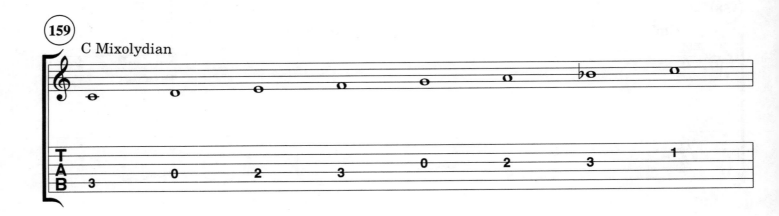

The Mixolydian mode also contains the same notes as a major scale beginning on the fifth degree. For example, E Mixolydian has the same notes as the A major scale.

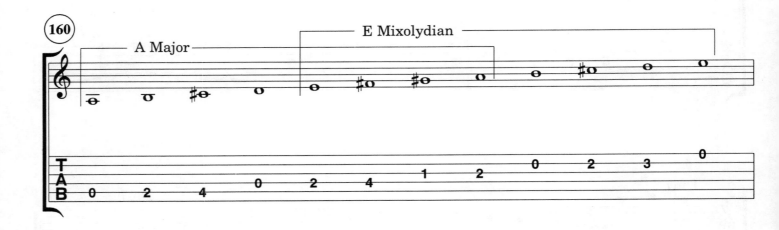

The most popular fingerings for the Mixolydian mode are shown below.

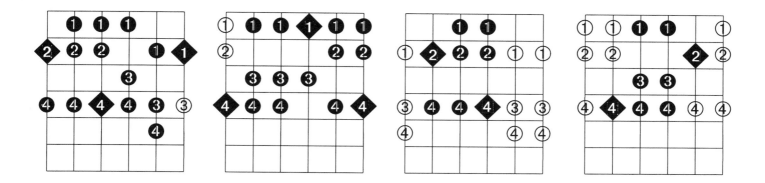

Because a seventh chord contains a flat seventh, the Mixolydian mode works great against a seventh chord. The name of the Mixolydian mode used will be the same letter name as the chord. For example, for D7, use D Mixolydian. The Mixolydian mode can also be used against other chords from the seventh chord family (i.e. 9, 11 and 13). Because seventh chords are used in the blues, it is common to use the Mixolydian mode to play a blues solo. Unlike using the blues scale where you could use the same scale to solo over all of the chords in the blues progression, you have to change the Mixolydian mode you are using each time a new chord is played.

Against the blues progression below, Mixolydian modes are used for the solo. Each time the chord changes, a new Mixolydian mode is used. For G7, use G Mixolydian. For C7, use C Mixolydian, and for D7, use D Mixolydian. The advantage of knowing several different fingerings is that you can change mode and not change position.

Practice the following solo which is a blues in G, and then create your own blues solos using the Mixolydian mode.

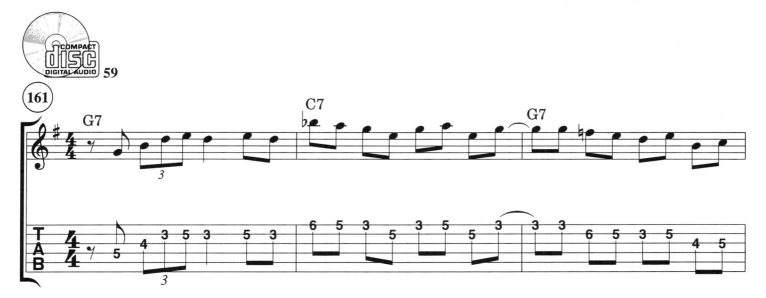

149

Combining Modes

Now that you know some of the modes and when and how to use them, it's time to start combining these modes to build solos. Remember, the Dorian mode can be used with minor chords, the Mixolydian mode is used with seventh chords, and the major scale (the Ionian mode) is used with major chords. If you have a chord progression which uses minor, seventh, and major type chords, by combining the different modes you can solo over the changes (the chord changes).

The following solos use the Dorian mode over the minor seventh chords, the Mixolydian mode over the seventh chords, and the Ionian mode (the major scale) over the major seventh chords. Notice how well the notes of the solo fit with the chords. Also, notice the letter name of the mode used is the same as the letter name of the chord for which it is used. For example, D Dorian over Dm7.

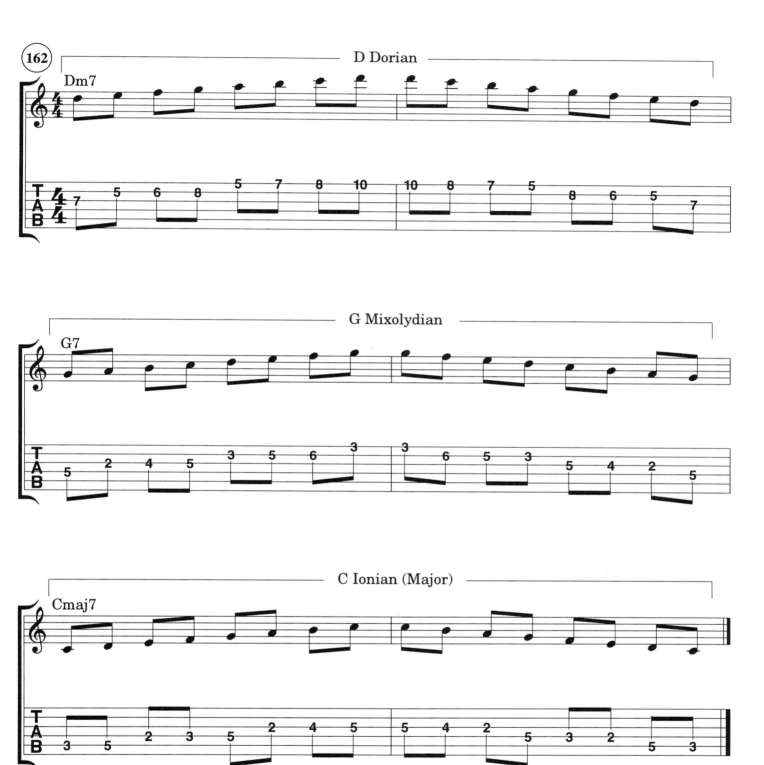

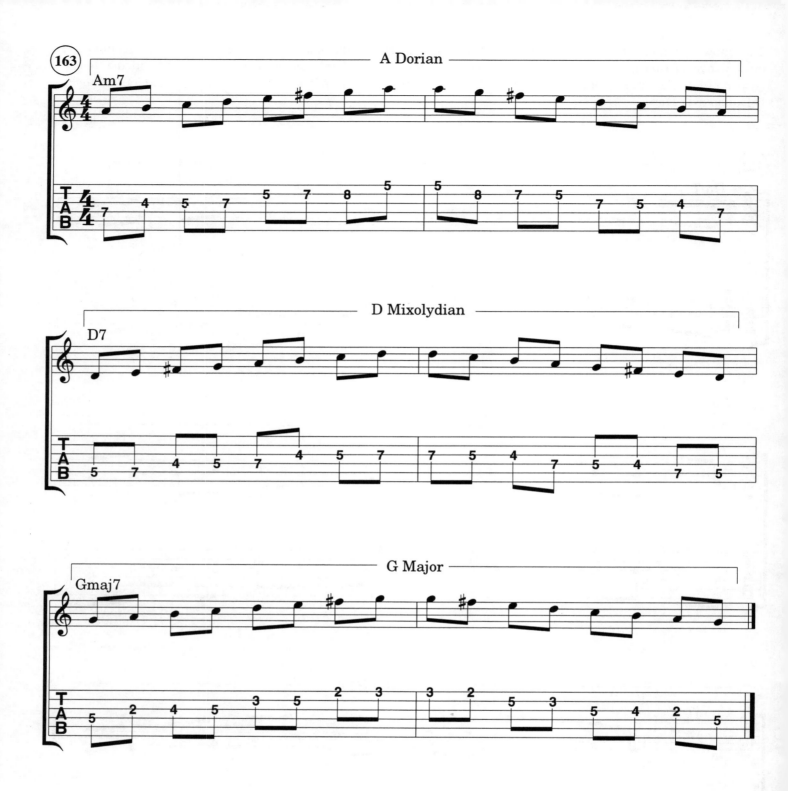

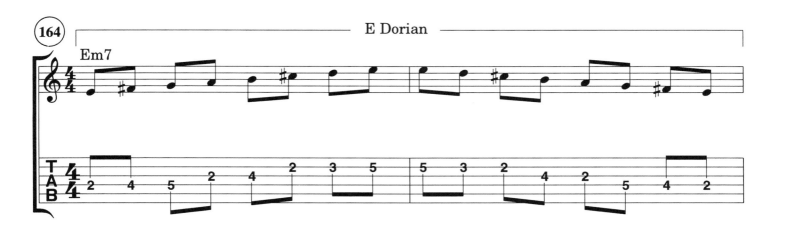

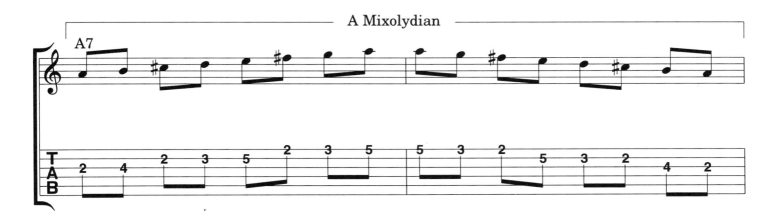

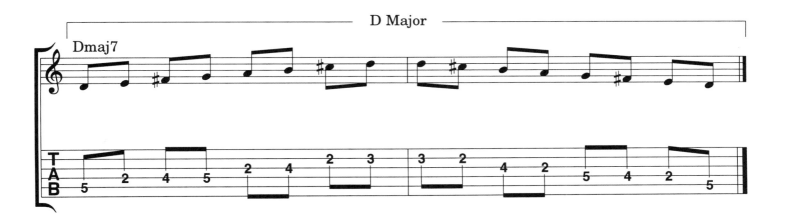

Improvising Over The ii-V-I Progression

The most common chord progression in all of jazz is the ii-V-I chord progression. Remember, the ii chord in any major key is built with its root on the second step of the major scale and is a minor-type chord. The V chord is built with its root on the fifth step of the scale and is usually a seventh chord (or any chord from the dominant chord family). The I chord is built with its root on the first step of the major scale and can be any major-type chord. The chart below shows the ii-V-I chords in the various keys.

ii	V	I (Key)
Dm	G7	C
Am	D7	G
Em	A7	D
Bm	E7	A
F♯m	B7	E
Gm	C7	F
Cm	F7	B♭
Fm	B♭7	E♭
B♭m	E♭7	A♭
C♯m	F♯7	B
E♭m	A♭7	D♭

In the following solos, the Dorian mode is used over the ii chord, the Mixolydian mode is used over the V chord, and the major scale is used over the I chord.

Practice soloing over the following examples which use ii-V-I progressions in various keys. Use Dorian modes over the minor-type chords, Mixolydian modes over the chords from the dominant seventh family, and major scales over the major-type chords. If you have the recording which goes with this book, improvise to the rhythm tracks for these examples. Another guitarist or keyboard player could also play these chords while you solo. The chords can be strummed four times in each measure or comp patterns can be used.

The following solo is written over the ii-V-I chord progression. In this example, the notes used in the solo come from the major scale of the I chord. As was explained earlier in this book, this process uses the tonal center concept to solo. Although one scale is used over a set of chords, notice how the strong beats (beats one and three) are chord tones. This is important and gives the solo a strong feeling of tonality and direction. Notice that by using the major scale of the key (the I chord), you end up using the Dorian mode over the minor seventh chords, the Mixolydian mode over the seventh chords, and the major scale over the major seventh chords.

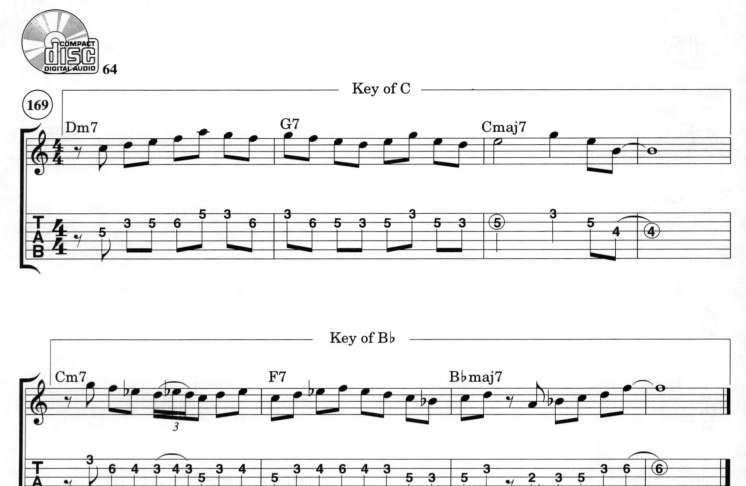

In the following example, the solo is written using the E Dorian mode for the ii chord (Em7), the A Mixolydian mode for the V chord (A13), and the D major scale for the I chord (Dmaj7). Notice the frequent use of chord tones on the heavy beats.

The ii-V-I chord progression is so commonly used in jazz that, when you see a minor-type chord, be alerted that it could well be the ii chord of the key. Knowing this can help you quickly determine what major scale can be used to improvise to the progression. For example, if you are soloing and you see an Em7 chord, it's very possible that you are in the key of D and the chord which follows the Em7 will be an A7 chord. When you see the Em7 chord, you could begin improvising using the D major scale and stay on that same scale for the next several chords of the progression.

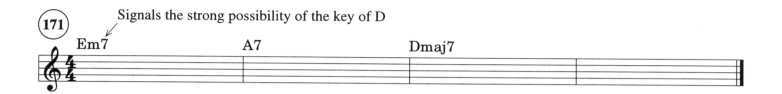

The ii-V-i chord progression is also commonly used in a minor key. In a minor key, the ii chord will often be a m7♭5. The V chord will usually be a chord from the dominant seventh family, and the i chord will be some type of a minor chord. For example, a common chord progression in the key of D minor would be, Em7♭5 to A7 to Dm7. The following examples are ii-V-i chord progressions in popular minor keys.

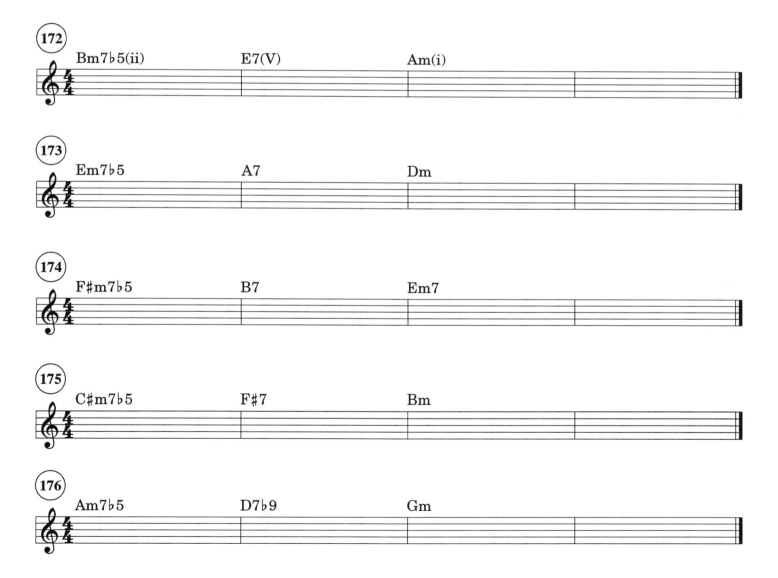

The following solo uses the A harmonic minor scale over the ii-V-i progression in the key of A minor.

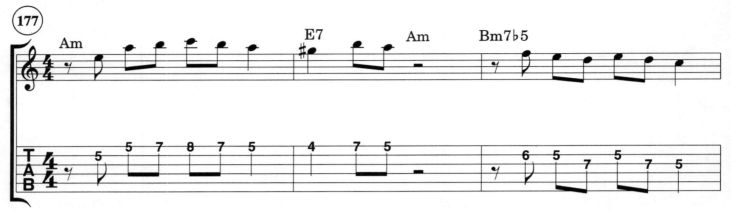

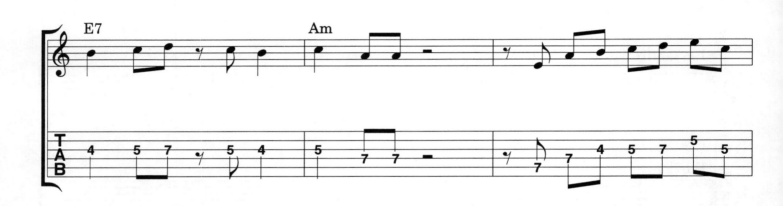

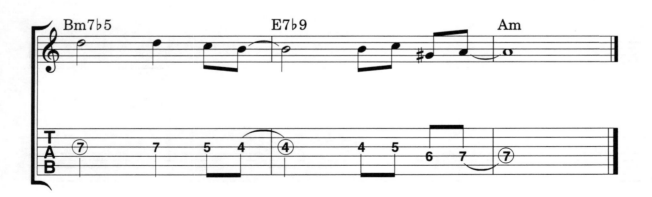

Lydian Mode

The Lydian mode is a major scale beginning on the fourth degree. For example, if you play the notes of a C major scale and begin on the F note, you will be playing the F Lydian mode. Another way of finding the Lydian mode is to play a major scale and raise the fourth degree. For example, to play the C Lydian mode, play the notes of a C major scale beginning on C and sharp the F's.

Shown below are the notes in the C Lydian mode.

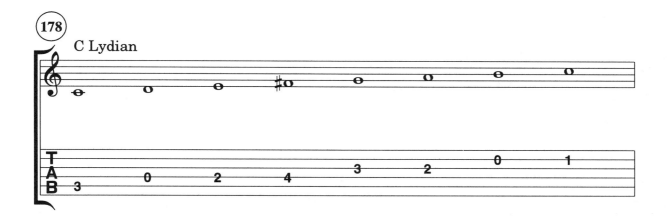

Drawn on the diagrams below are some common fingerings for the Lydian mode.

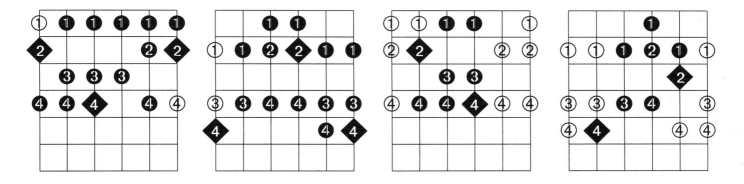

This mode can be used to improvise and create melodies for major type chords. It is especially effective against the maj7 and maj7♯11 chords.

The following solo uses the C Lydian mode over the Cmaj7 chord and B♭ Lydian over the B♭maj7 chord. Notice the letter name of the Lydian mode which is used should be the same as the letter name of the chord with which it is used.

The next solo uses the A Dorian mode against the Am7 chord, the D Mixolydian mode against the D7th chord, and the G Lydian mode against the Gmaj7 and the Gmaj7#11 chords.

Aeolian Mode

The Aeolian mode is a major scale beginning on the sixth degree. For example, D Aeolian contains the same notes as the F major scale. The Aeolian mode contains the same notes as the natural minor scale with the same letter name. A Aeolian is the same as A natural minor.

The notes for the A Aeolian mode are shown below.

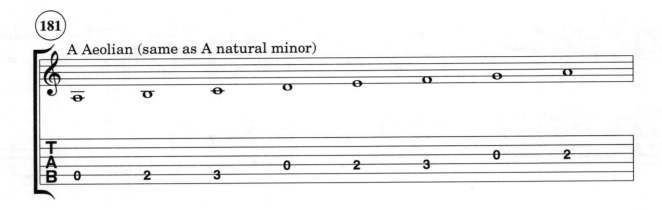

Drawn below are four of the common fingerings for the Aeolian mode.

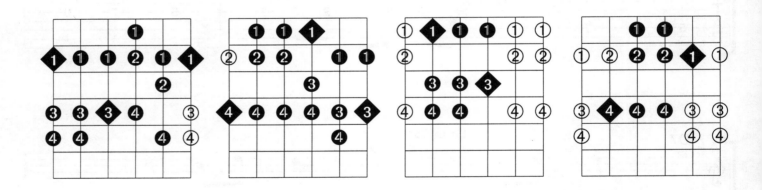

The Aeolian mode can be used to improvise to minor-type chords. For example, the A Aeolian mode could be used to improvise to Am7. The following example uses the D Aeolian mode (D Aeolian contains the same notes a D natural minor) over the Dm7 chord.

Phrygian Mode

The Phrygian mode contains the same notes as the major scale beginning on the third step, or degree. For example, E Phrygian = C major. The notes of the E Phrygian mode are shown below.

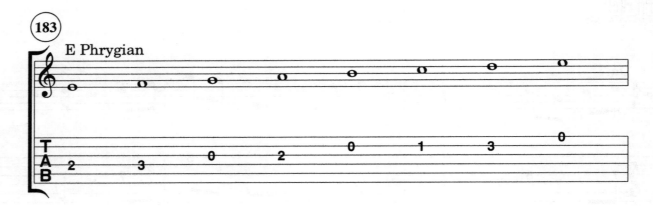

Drawn on the following diagrams are some of the common fingerings for the Phrygian mode.

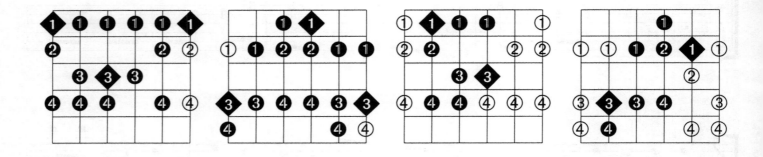

The Phrygian mode works well with minor-type chords. The following solo uses the A Phrygian mode over an A minor chord.

69

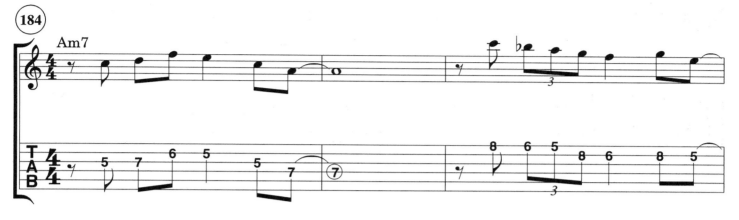

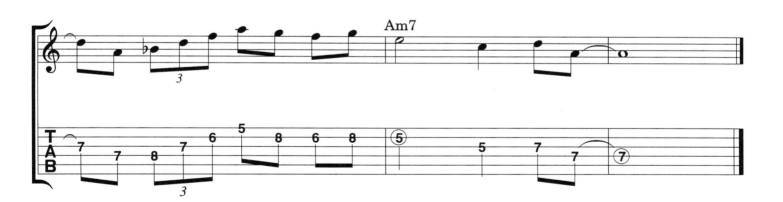

The Phrygian mode has a very Spanish/flamenco sound when used over a major chord. The Phrygian mode used to get this sound should have the same letter name as the major chord over which it is used. The next example uses the E Phrygian mode over an E major chord of the same letter name. Notice the Spanish quality.

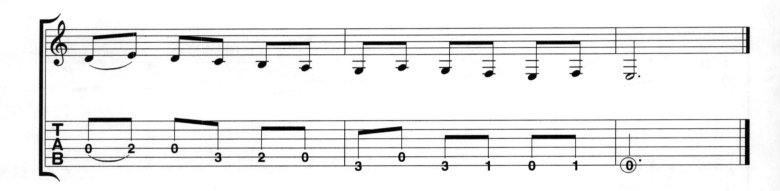

Locrian Mode

The Locrian mode is a major scale beginning on the seventh degree. For example, the B Locrian mode would contain the same notes as the C major scale beginning and ending on a B note. Written below are the notes in the B Locrian mode.

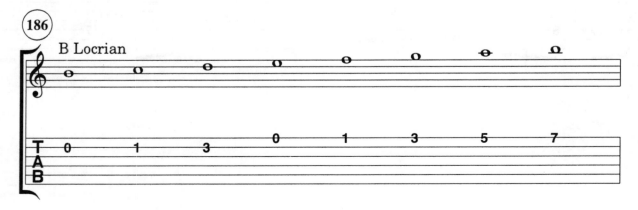

Drawn below are four of the fingerings for the Locrian mode. Two have roots on the sixth string and two have roots on the fifth string.

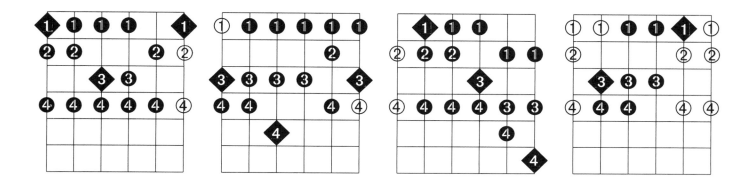

A common place to use the Locrian mode is with the m7♭5 (half diminished) chord. For example, over a Bm7♭5 chord use the B Locrian mode. A quick way to think of this would be: when you are improvising to a m7♭5 chord, play the major scale which is 1/2 step (one fret) higher than the name of the chord. Using the major scale in this way would be the same as using the Locrian mode.

Practice the following solo which uses the B Locrian mode over the Bm7♭5 chord and D Locrian over the Dm7♭5 chord.

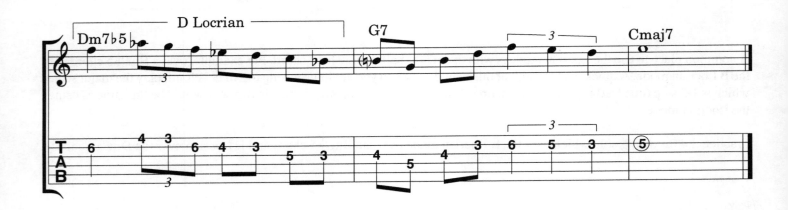

Super Locrian Mode

The Super Locrian mode is a major scale with a root, ♭2, ♭3, ♭4, ♭5, ♭6, and ♭7. A much more convenient way to think of the Super Locrian mode would be to think of the melodic minor scale which is 1/2 step above the letter name of the Super Locrian mode which you want to play. For example, G Super Locrian contains the same notes as A♭ melodic minor. D Super Locrian contains the same notes as E♭ melodic minor. The Super Locrian mode is used to improvise against 7th chords and other embellishments of the 7th chord (9th, 13, etc.). The Super Locrian mode is particularly effective when improvising against altered 7th chords (7♭5, 7♭5♯9, etc.).

Written below are the notes in the C Super Locrian mode. The same notes are in the D♭ melodic minor scale.

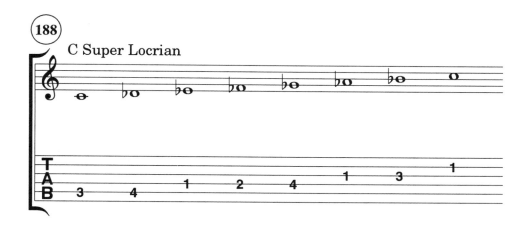

The fingerings for the Super Locrian mode are drawn below.

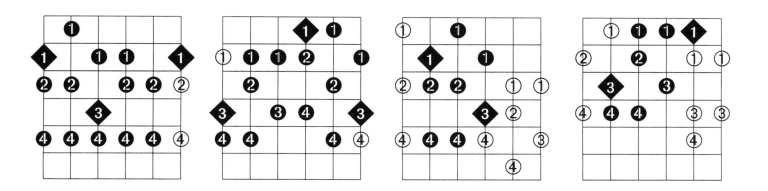

171

Practice the following solo which uses the G Super Locrian mode over the G7♭9 chord. The G Super Locrian mode contains the same notes as the A♭ melodic minor scale. Again, notice that chord tones are played on heavy beats.

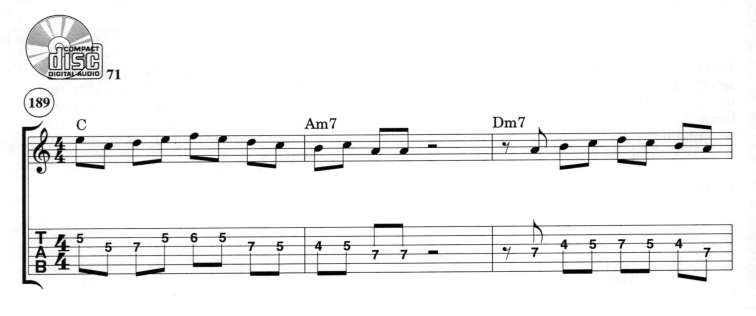

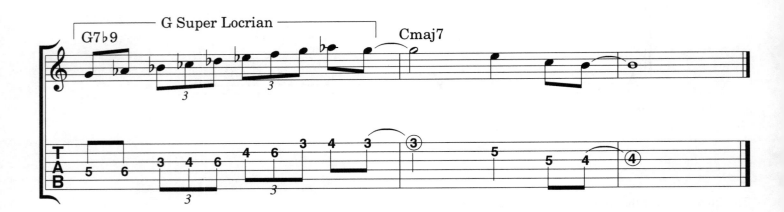

Arpeggios

The term *arpeggio* refers to playing a broken chord, or playing the notes of a chord one at a time rather than simultaneously. Because each note you are playing is a note from the chord, each note will sound harmonically correct with the chord. Using arpeggios in your improvisation is one of the most important concepts of improvisation you will learn. Arpeggios are essential. Unlike using scales, where the same scale could be used to improvise over a series of chords, when you use arpeggios, the arpeggio has to change each time the chord changes. The name of the arpeggio used should match the name of the chord. Against a Dm7 chord, you would play a Dm7 arpeggio, and against a B♭7 chord you would use a B♭7 arpeggio.

The following diagrams show common fingerings for the basic arpeggios. The types of chords are written across the top. The "R" is written next to the roots in the patterns. The chart above the diagrams shows the fret locations of the roots on strings six, five, and four.

Chart for Locating Roots

Fret Number – – – – –	0	1	2	3	4	5	6	7	8	9	10	11	12
Sixth String Root Name	E	F		G		A		B	C		D		E
Fifth String Root Name	A		B	C		D		E	F		G		A
Fourth String Root Name	D		E	F		G		A		B	C		D

Arpeggio Patterns

With the dim arpeggio, every note can be the root.

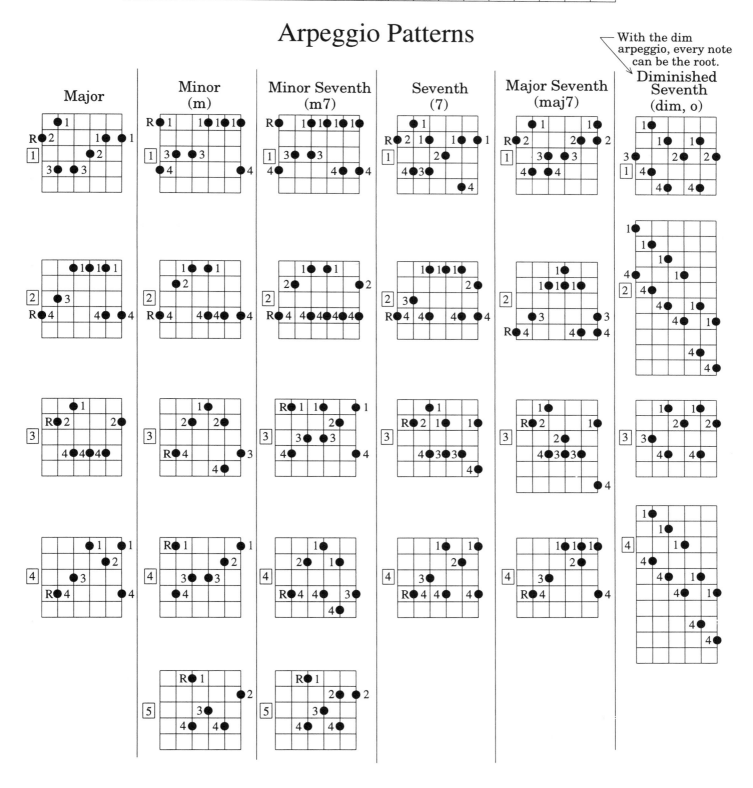

173

Practice all of these patterns. Notice where the chord is in relationship to the arpeggio pattern. For example, on the diagrams below are the G7 chord and the G7 arpeggio. Notice the notes of the arpeggio are contained in the chord pattern.

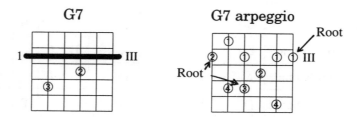

In the following exercise, play the m7 arpeggio with the root on the fifth string going from the low string to the high and then returning to the low strings. The arpeggio pattern which is used is pattern ③ of the minor seventh arpeggio patterns found on the previous page.

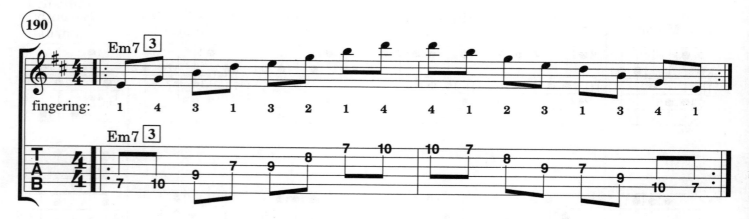

Play the minor seventh arpeggio with the root on the fifth string from low notes to high, and then return the pattern down one-half step from high notes to low. Continue moving the minor seventh arpeggio down one-half step each time the pattern is completed. This exercise should be practiced with each arpeggio pattern.

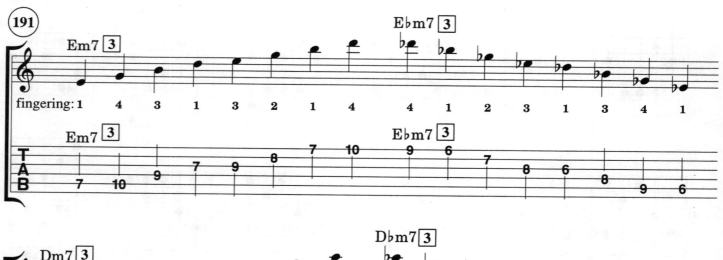

174

The following exercise uses the minor seventh arpeggio 1 with the root on the sixth string.

In the following exercises, the arpeggios of several different chords are connected. The pattern which is being used is indicated in a box next to the chord name. Notice in these exercises, the chords which are being arpeggiated are the ii-V-I chords in the keys of G and D.

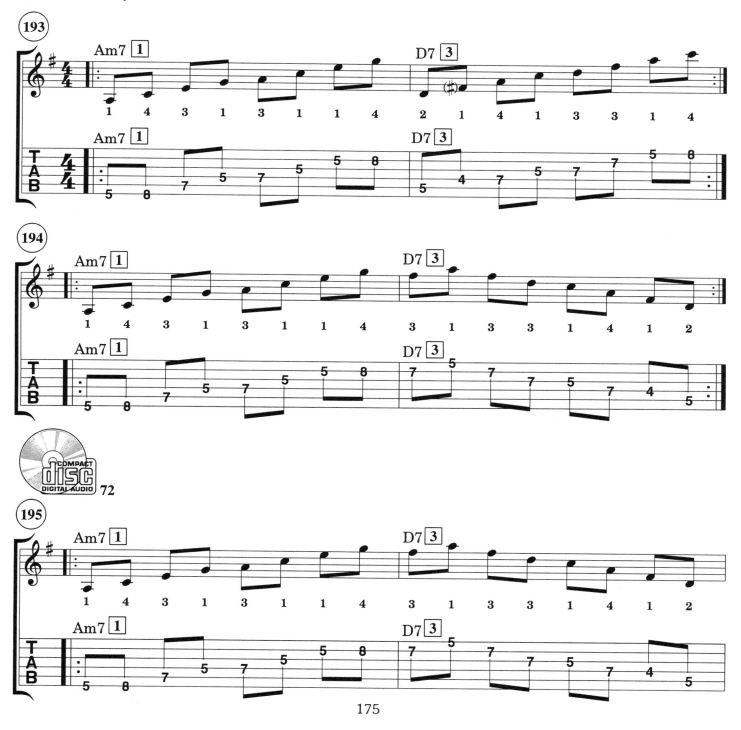

175

176

The next exercise will help you learn to connect arpeggio patterns. Play the arpeggio pattern for the type of chord which is written. The pattern to be used is indicated in the box. The arrow shows the direction in which the notes are to be played (➚ indicates low notes to high notes). For example,

Em7
[3] ➚

would mean to play the m7 pattern No. 3 with the root on E. The upward arrow means to play the notes from low to high (fifth string to first string).

Practice connecting the following arpeggios. The arpeggio diagrams with their numbers can be found near the beginning of this chapter.

Arpeggio Connections

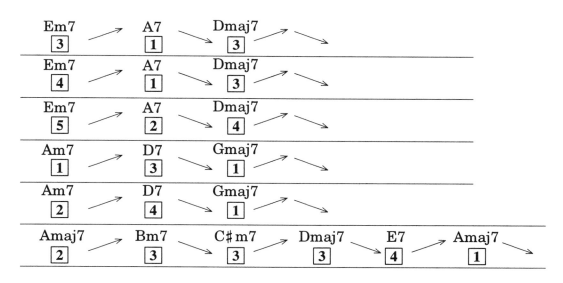

Practice playing arpeggios to the following progression. You decide which arpeggio to use. When playing an arpeggio, you don't have to begin with the top or bottom note. You can arpeggiate a chord by starting anywhere in the pattern. However, starting with the lowest or highest note is a good practice at first. Also, practice playing only eighth-note rhythms. In 4/4, play eight notes to the measure. After that, experiment with other rhythms.

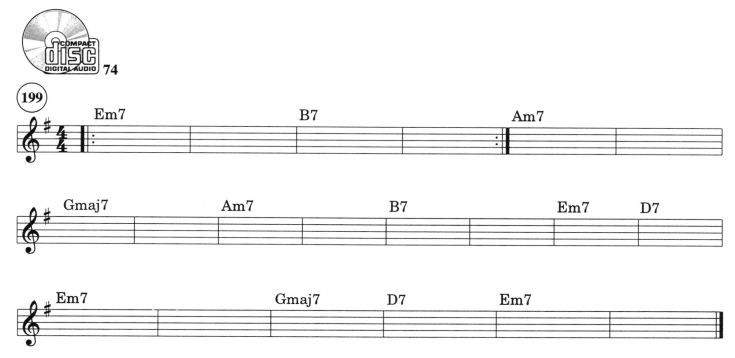

A good exercise to practice would be to take a jazz standard and arpeggiate, in time, all of the chords. The next example shows how this could be done to the chord changes of the standard, *All The Things You Are*.

The following solos use a combination of arpeggios and scales. So they can be seen easily, the arpeggios have been circled. The scales which are used are either the blues scale, the key scale (tonal center), or modes which you have learned.

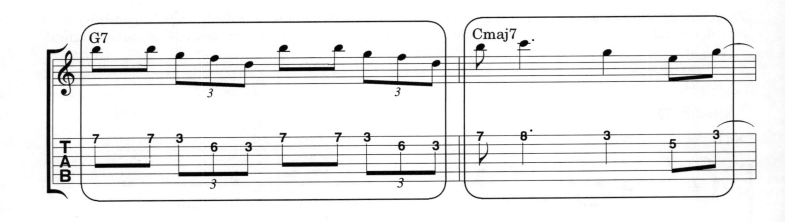

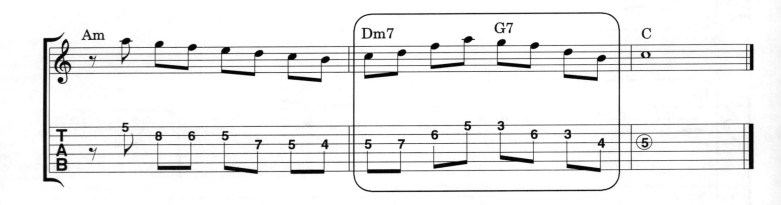

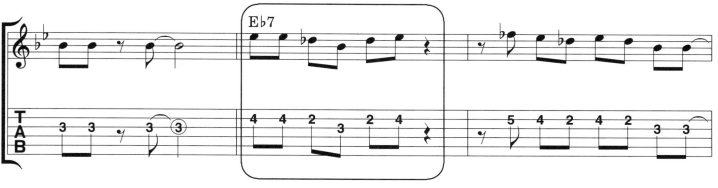

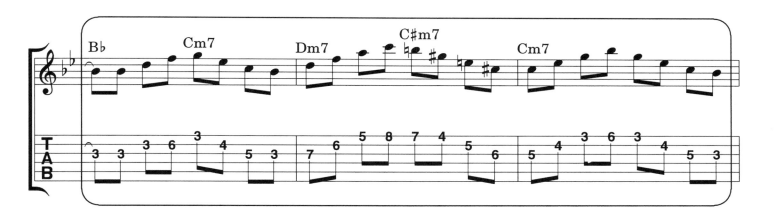

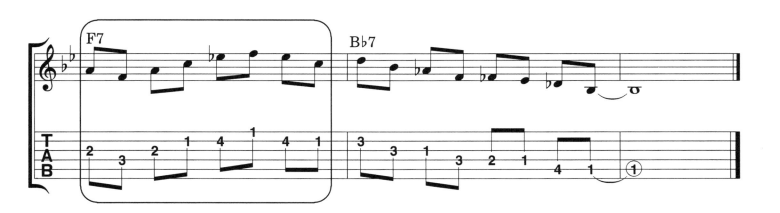

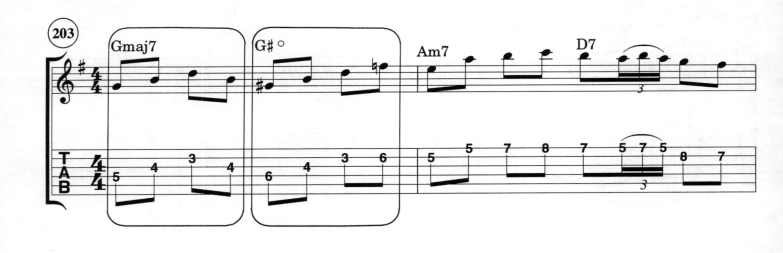

If the chord you want to arpeggiate is not one of the arpeggio patterns found in this book, you can reduce the chord to one you can arpeggiate. For example, if the chord you want to arpeggiate is G13, you could use an arpeggio pattern for the G7 chord like the one below in place of G13.

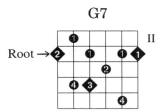

To build arpeggios of chords for which the arpeggio patterns are not drawn in this book, you can add extra notes (i.e. 9, 13, ♭5, ♯9, etc.) to the basic arpeggio patterns. For example, if you want to arpeggiate a C9 chord, start with the C7 arpeggio like the one drawn below.

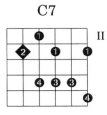

Next, locate the extra notes needed to change C7 to C9. In this case, the ninth has to be added to C7 to make it C9. The diagram below shows where the ninth is located in relation to the C7 chord and the C7 arpeggio pattern.

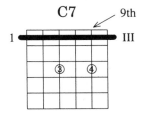   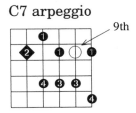

183

To arpeggiate the C9 chord, add the ninth to the C7 arpeggio.

C9 arpeggio

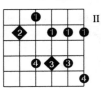

This technique can be used to build all arpeggio patterns. To build altered chord arpeggios (i.e. D7#5b9), the process is the same. For example, if you want to arpeggiate G7b9, begin with the G7 arpeggio.

G7

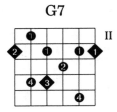

Next, locate the b9 in relation to the G7 chord and arpeggio pattern.

G7

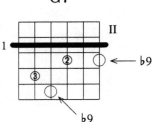

G7 arpeggio

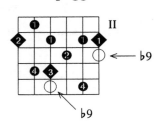

Finally, add the ♭9 into the arpeggio pattern. The G7♭9 arpeggio pattern is drawn below.

G7♭9 arpeggio

If you are not sure where the intervals are located around the chord, refer to the section in this book on "Chord Construction." There you will find the locations of all the intervals around the chord patterns.

The next solo contains arpeggios which are modifications of the arpeggio patterns found in this book. The sections in the solo where arpeggios are played have been circled and the arpeggio patterns are drawn above the measures in which they are used.

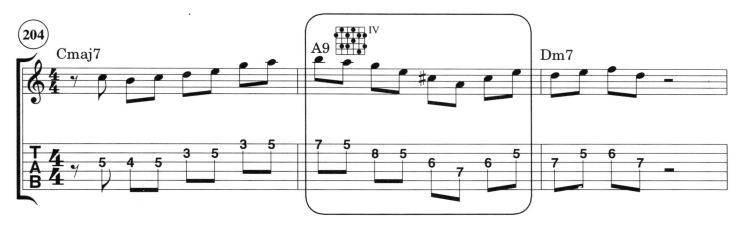

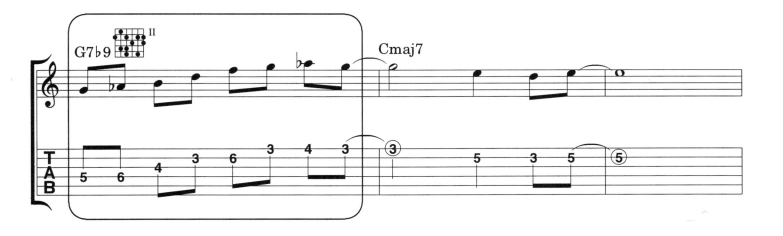

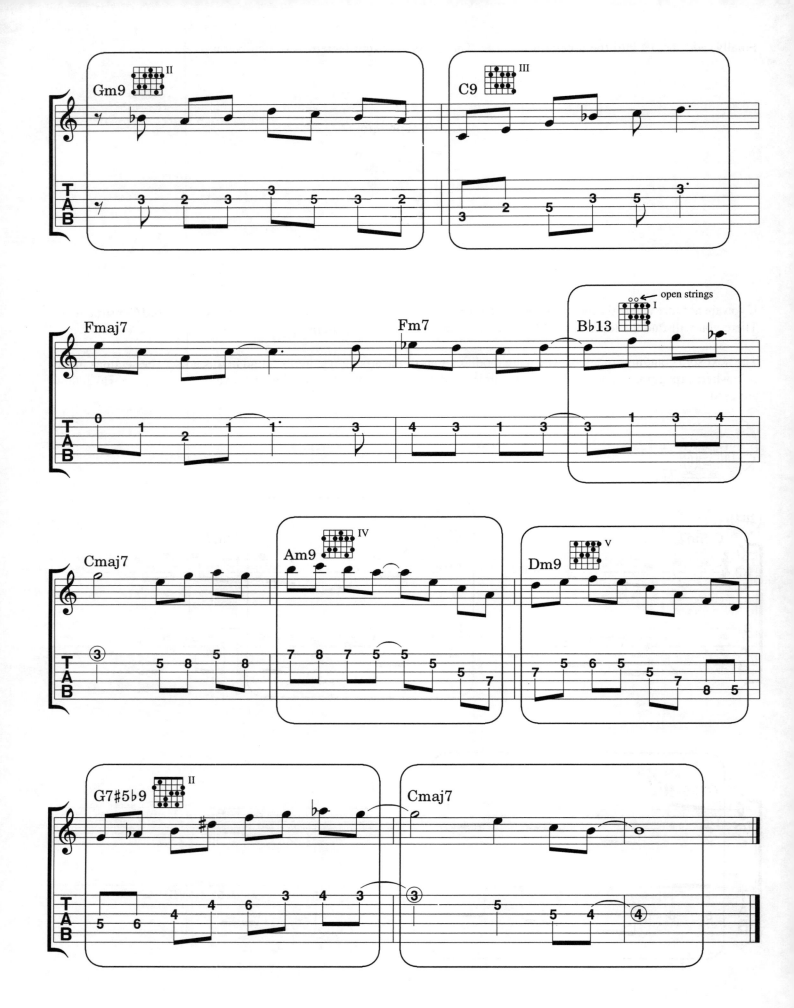

Arpeggio Sequences

Arpeggios can be sequenced in the same way in which scales can be sequenced. As with the scales, a pattern of notes is established and then the pattern is repeated ascending or descending the arpeggio.

Written below are several common arpeggio sequence patterns. These sequence patterns are written for an Em7 chord but they can be memorized and transposed to fit any letter name chord of any type. To do this, the patterns should be learned by thinking of the order of the notes in the arpeggio. For example, a sequence pattern may begin on the first note of the arpeggio, go up three notes in the arpeggio pattern, and then begin on the second note of the arpeggio and go up another three notes of the arpeggio. This sequence is then repeated through all of the notes in the arpeggio.

After you learn and have applied these sequences, create your own sequences using arpeggio patterns.

Although the sequences below begin on the root of the chord, sequences can begin and end on any note in the arpeggio.

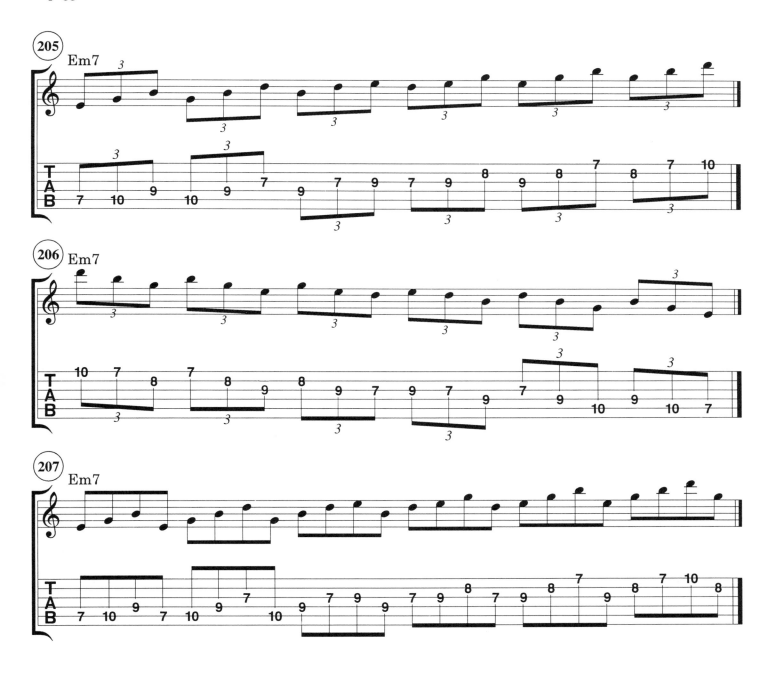

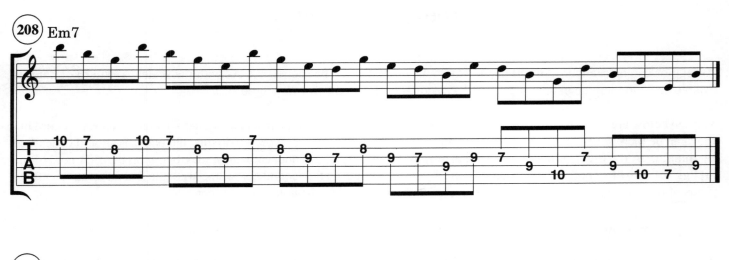

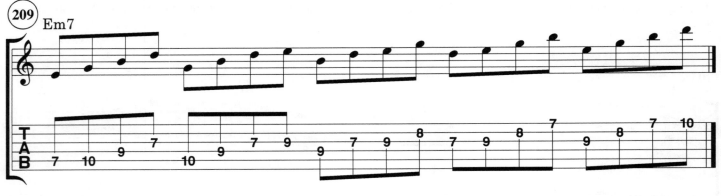

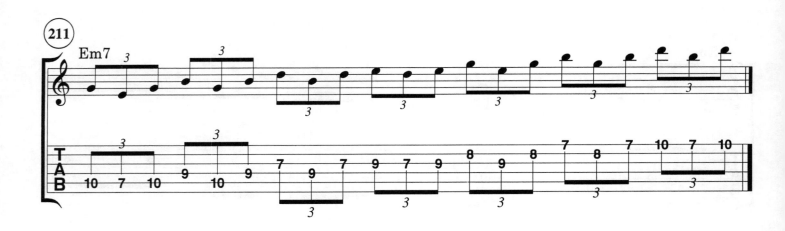

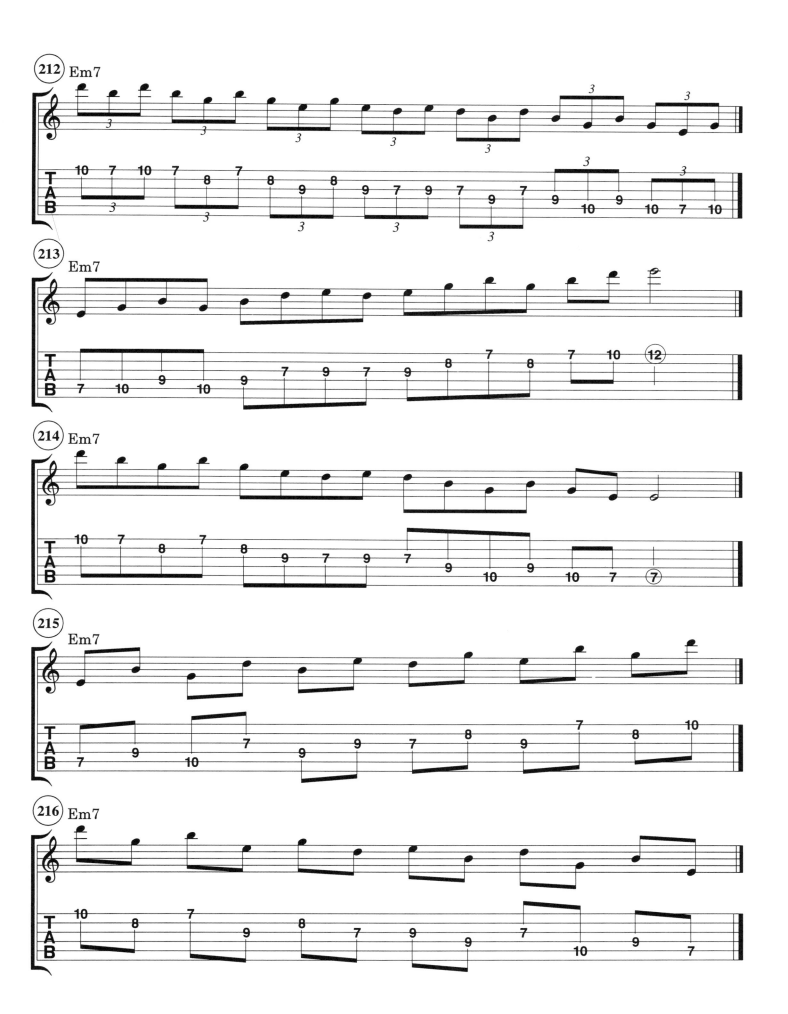

The following solo contains arpeggio sequences. They are usually easy to spot because of the evenness of the note spacing. The sequences in this solo have been circled to make them easy to locate.

Targeting

Targeting is a term which refers to playing notes around chord tones (the notes in a chord) and then playing the chord tone. In a way, you are "zeroing in" on the notes of the chord. Once you decide how to target a chord tone, the same approach is used to target all of the notes of the chord. For example, one method of targeting the notes of an Am chord would be to select any Am chord form and play a note in the chord followed by a note which is one fret below the chord tone; then,

Am

play the chord tone again. The following shows how this method of targeting is done. The circled dot shows the chord tone, and the empty circle shows the note played next to the chord tone.

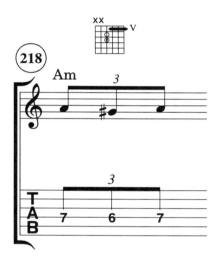

Repeat this pattern (chord tone–one fret below–chord tone) on each note of the chord. Written below is an example of this targeting pattern on an Am chord in the fifth fret. Again, on the diagram, the dots indicate the chord tones and circles show the notes played around the chord tones.

This same targeting pattern can be used with any chord form. For example, written below is the same targeting pattern only this time it is used with a Dm chord in the fifth fret.

The diagrams below show how the notes of the Am and Dm chords can be targeted. The solid dots indicate the chord tones, and the circles indicate the notes that are played around the chord tones.

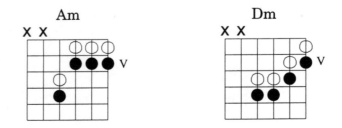

The following examples are targeting patterns which will work with the Am chord in the fifth fret. So they can be seen easily, the chord tones have been circled in standard notation and tablature. These target patterns can be used with any chord form of any chord type. The first targeting pattern below consists of playing 1/2 step (1 fret) below the chord tone and then the chord tone.

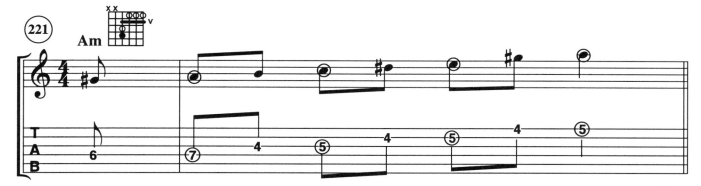

The targeting example below uses the technique of playing 1/2 step below the chord tone, 1/2 step above the chord tone, and then the chord tone.

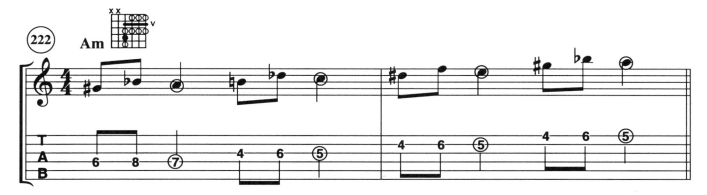

In the next targeting example, the order and the notes used in the pattern are: 1/2 step below the chord tone, 1 whole step (two frets) above the chord tone, 1/2 step above the chord tone, and then the chord tone.

The following is a popular targeting pattern which consists of playing one scale step above the chord tone, followed by 1/2 step below the chord tone, and then the chord tone. The example below shows this targeting technique with a G chord in the third fret.

The next solo uses targeting with several of the chords. The sections where targeting occurs have been circled. The chord patterns which are being used for the targeting are drawn above the measures.

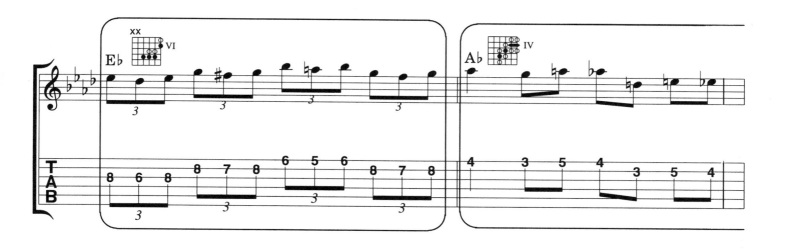

Guide Tones

Guide tones are notes which connect chords smoothly (usually by half step or whole step). Guide tones are usually played where one chord ends and a new chord begins. A guide tone is the last note played in the improvisation over a chord before the chord changes. Guide tones are usually 1/2 step away from the notes they are approaching. In the example below, the guide tones have been circled.

195

One of the most common guide tones is for the seventh of one chord to lead to the third of the next chord. In this case, the seventh of the chord is the guide tone. The following example shows this. The guide tones have been circled. Notice how the guide tones introduce a chord change.

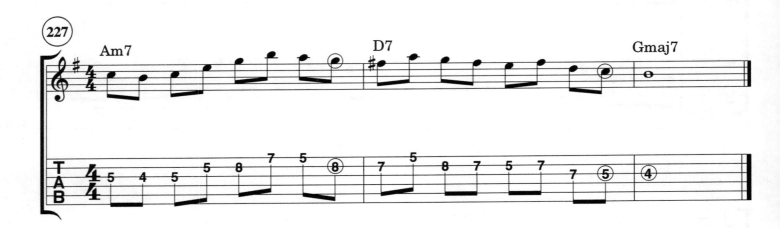

The third of one chord may also lead to the seventh of the next chord. In this case, the third of the chord is the guide tone. The next example shows this.

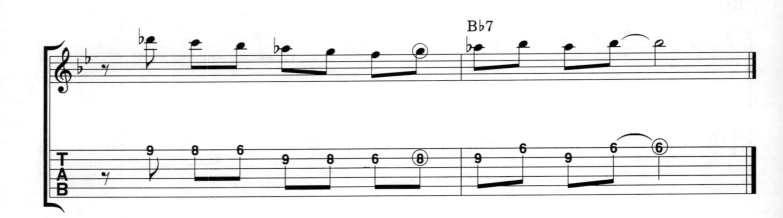

The guitar is a unique instrument for seeing guide tones. It is easy to visualize the fingering of a particular chord and see how the seventh leads to the third of the next chord and vice versa. On the diagrams below, you can see how the notes in the different chords connect. The guide tones and the notes to which they lead have been circled.

Although the patterns are drawn for specific chord letter names, they can be moved up or down the neck as long as the fret relationship between the two chord forms remains the same.

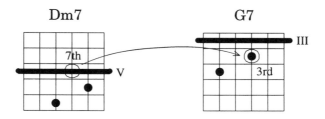

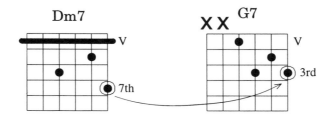

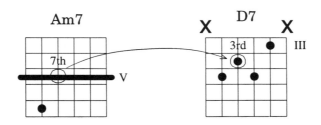

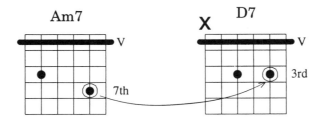

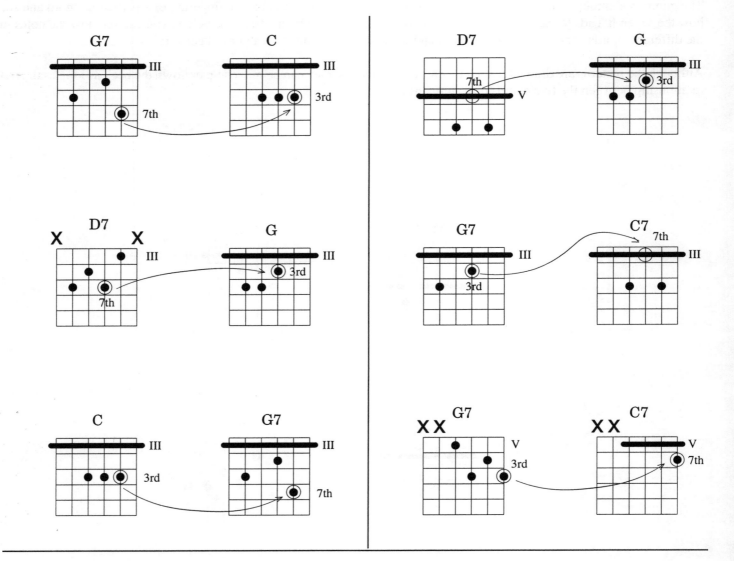

It is also possible for the notes on each string of a chord to be guide tones to the chord notes on the same string of the next chord. When used in this manner, the guide tones may, or may not, be 1/2 step away from the notes they are approaching. Drawn below are the diagrams of the A7 and D7 chords. The arrows show how the notes on each string of the A7 chord could connect and be used as guide tones to the notes on the same strings of a D7 chord. Notice some of the notes in the A7 are the same as some of the notes in a D7. This same method of finding guide tones can be used to connect any two chords.

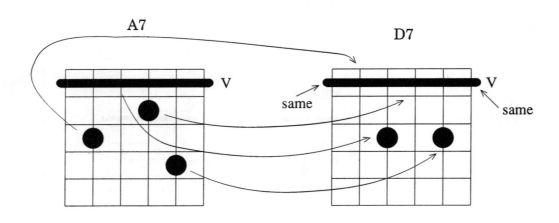

The following solo is a blues in A. The guide tones have been circled. You can see that the guide tones are played when the chords change. Above the guide tones are drawn the chord diagrams containing the guide tones. The circles in the diagrams indicate the guide tones and the notes to which they are leading. Notice how the notes which are played at the end of a chord and the beginning of a new chord are on the same string.

The next example is a ii-V-I progression in the key of C. Again, guide tones have been used to connect the chords. The guide tones have been circled. On the diagrams above the measures, the circles show guide tones and the notes to which they are leading.

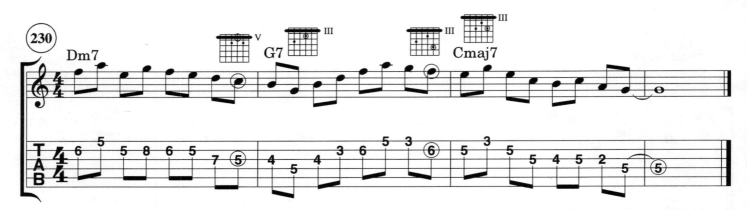

Guide tones do not have to be chord tones or notes from the key scale. Guide tones can simply be notes which are 1/2 step (one fret) away from the chord tone to which they are leading. The next solo uses this type of guide tone. Again, so they can be easily seen the guide tones have been circled.

200

In the next example, the guide tones have been written. Write the rest of the solo around the guide tones. In measure one, the lighter notes are an example of what you will be writing in the other measures. Use scales, modes, and arpeggios for the notes of the solo. Remember, the guide tones are one fret away from the note which follows them. Also, the note which follows a guide tone will probably be a note in the new chord.

Phrasing

The term *phrasing* refers to how rhythms are grouped. Phrases can be very short (less than one measure) or long. Whether or not a solo swings or has "a good feel" to it can be dependent on the use of good phrases. An excellent way to learn how to phrase would be to imitate melodies. This means to play the same rhythm as the original melody, only use your own improvised notes. For example, written below is a melody we will use as the foundation for the improvisation. Practice playing this melody.

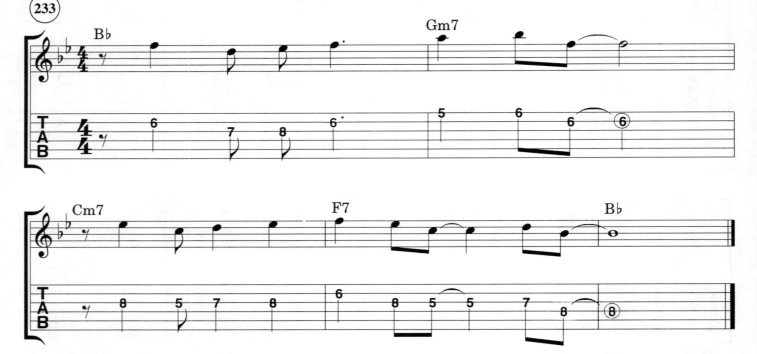

In the next example, notice that the same rhythms and chords have been used. The pauses come in the same place but the melody notes are different. This is an improvisation to the previous melody. The improvisation uses notes from the B♭ major scale.

Practice taking the melody to a popular jazz standard and write your own solo using the same rhythms as the original melody. It cannot be emphasized enough that the key to learning good phrasing is to **write out your solos.** Writing your solos allows you to slow your thinking and focus on the correct rhythms and notes. After you have written several solos, eventually your skills will develop to the point where you instinctively play well thought-out solos. You can use tonal centers, scales, modes, arpeggios, and guide tones in the solo.

Another way of learning how to phrase is to practice common rhythms used in jazz and then combine these rhythms to form phrases.

Written below are many rhythms which are commonly used in jazz. All of these rhythms are in 4/4. Playing a C note, practice each rhythm separately. The reason for holding one note is because you want to focus on the rhythms rather than which notes to play.

To get a good jazz swing feel, when two eighth notes are connected, accent the second note (♪♪).

Also, any note which precedes or follows a rest should be accented (⁊ ♩. ♫⁊ | ♫♩ ⁊) .

If you have the recording which goes with this book, hold a C note and practice these rhythms with the rhythm track. If you don't have the recording, record yourself of have another guitarist play any chord containing a C note while you play the rhythms with the one note. We will use other notes later.

After you play the rhythms separately, combine two or more of them to form phrases. The next examples show how this is done. The numbers corresponding to the rhythms being used are written above the measures.

235

(#4)   (#6)

236

(#1)   (#18)

237

(#28)   (#29)

238

(#4)   (#6)

239

(#16)   (#1)

240

(#22)   (#33)

Next, combine these rhythms to form phrases. Rather than stay on one note, use scales and/or arpeggios while playing the rhythms. The next example shows how this is done. The number of the rhythm used is written above the measure. After you play these notes, create your own solos to the same chord changes.

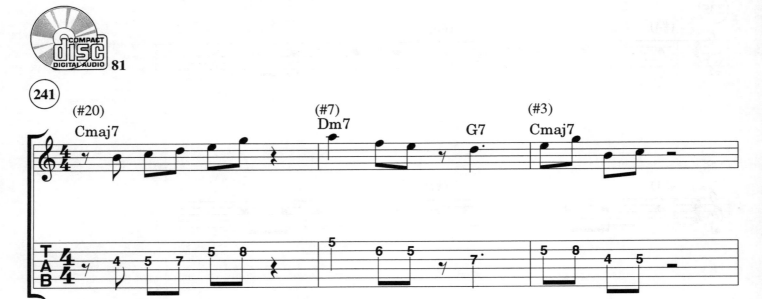

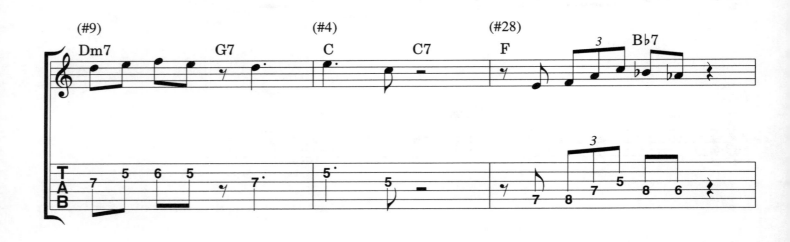

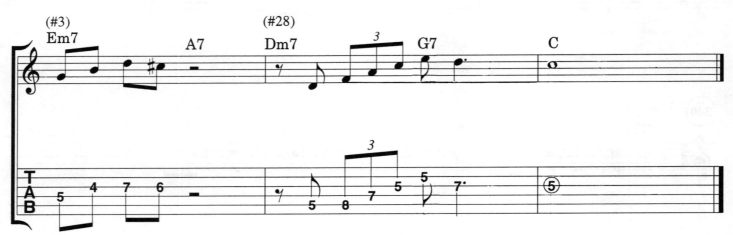

Now that you have combined the rhythms, practice playing one or more measures containing a series of eighth notes and then one or more of the jazz rhythms to create a longer phrase. The following examples show how this is done. The number of the rhythm used is written above the measure.

The following solo contains some common jazz rhythms. The numbers of the jazz rhythms used from pages 203–204 of this book are written above the measures in parentheses.

On the staves below, write your own solo using a series of eighth notes and one- or two-measure jazz rhythms.

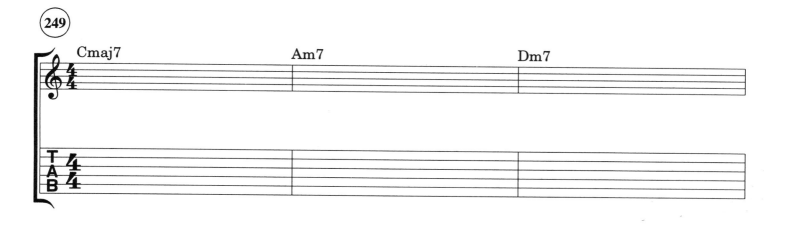

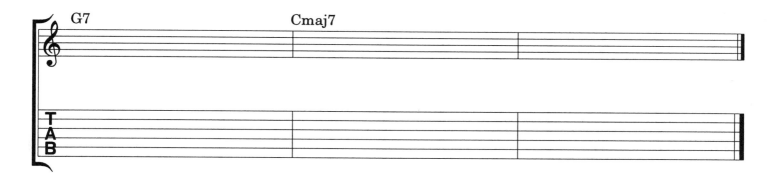

Constructing A Solo

Now you should know what notes can be used in your improvisations and how to build a phrase. In this section of the book, a method will be presented to show how a solo could be built. We are going to build a solo over the following progression.

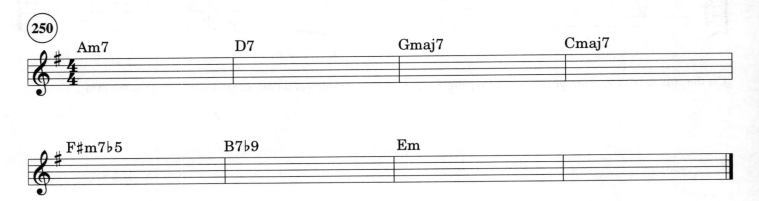

First, play one note per measure. Make sure the note is a chord tone. The following is an example of this. Play the written notes and then try playing different chord tones of your choice. After you play these written examples, play different chord tones of your choice over the same chord changes.

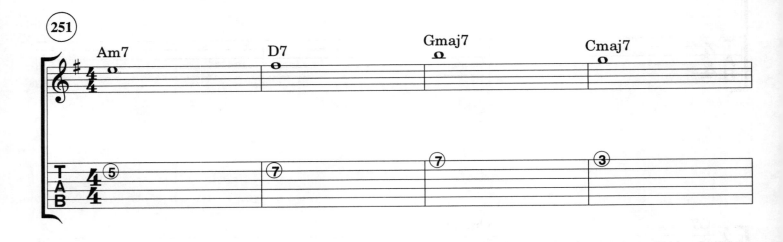

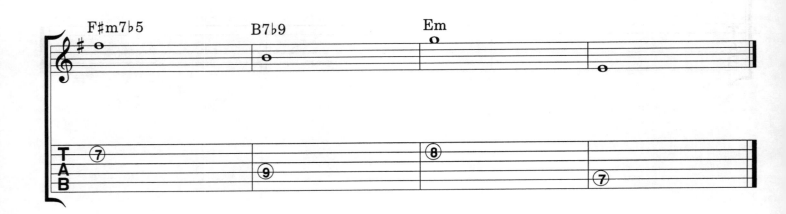

Next, play two notes per measure. Keep the one note per measure from the previous example and add another on beat three of each measure. The new note should also be a chord tone. Beats one and three are important beats harmonically. Don't be afraid to have wide intervals between the notes or play the same note twice. The spaces between the notes will be filled as you go through more steps in building the solo.

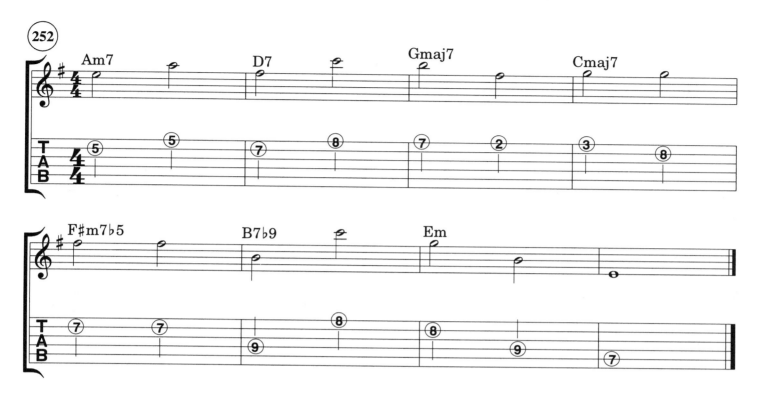

Next, keep the notes you played on beats one and three and add notes on beats two and four. Beat one should be a chord tone, and if possible, so should beat three. Beats two and four can be scale notes from the major scale of the key, arpeggio notes, from a mode, or guide tones. To assist you in finding the scales which can be used, the name of the tonal center (key)is circled and written above the chord changes.

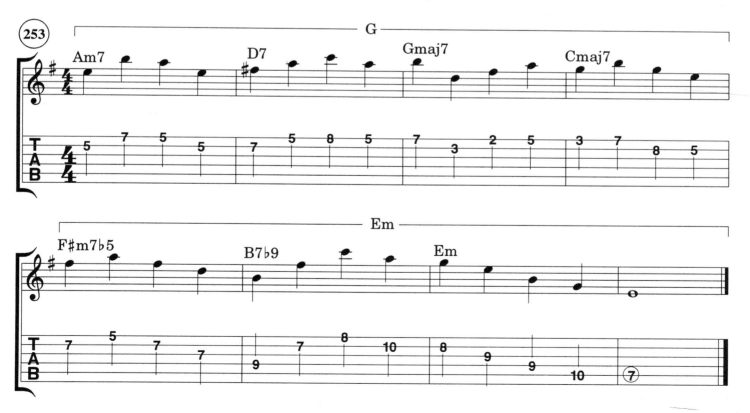

Next, play eight notes per measure. Keep the four notes you played in the last example and add notes on the off beats. Again, beat one should be a chord tone. The solo will have good direction if beat one and the first beat of each new chord are chord tones. Notice the use of guide tones in the example below. It may be difficult to keep all four notes from the previous example. The most important note to focus on is the one which is played on the first beat of the measure or the first beat of a new chord tone. Try to have this note be a chord tone.

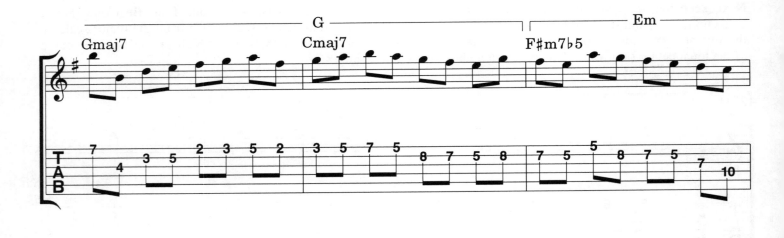

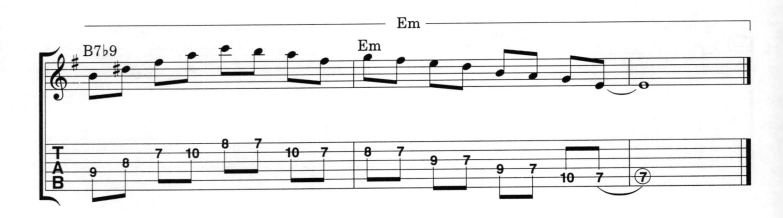

Finally, using a combination of eighth notes and jazz rhythms, construct your solo. Notice the final solo contains many of the original notes from the step-by-step process.

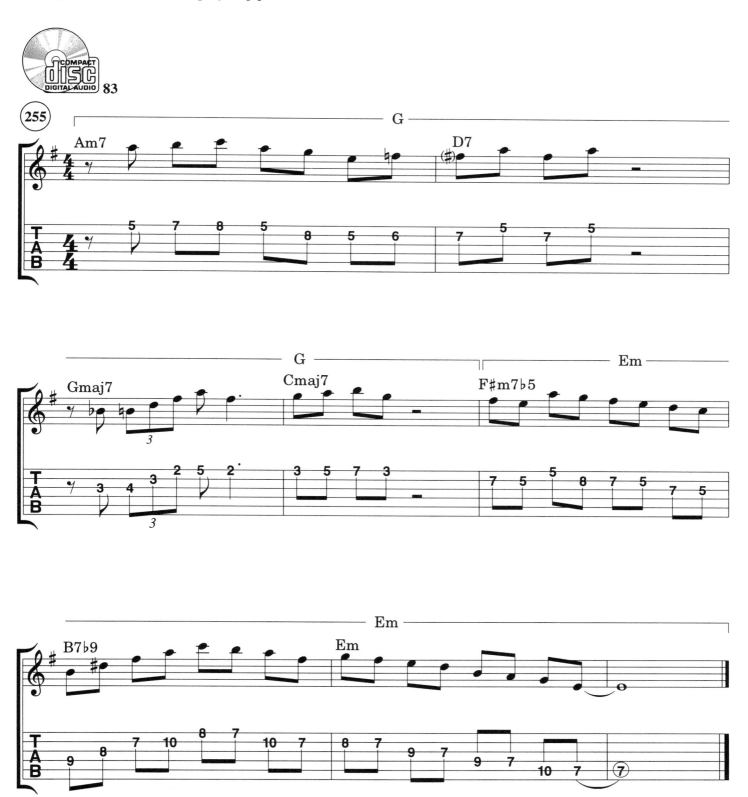

Write out the changes to a jazz standard and, using the steps you have just gone through, construct a solo to the changes. Try to have the first notes of the measures and the first notes of each new chord change be chord tones. Be sure to write your solo. Writing your solo slows down your thought process and helps you to play better notes. As a result of writing your solos, you will eventually play solos spontaneously which are harmonically and rhythmically well thought out.

Written below are some other helpful tips and considerations to make when building an improvised solo.

1. Use scales, arpeggios, modes, and guide tones.

2. Do not repeat the same notes one after the other.

3. Avoid large skips. The skip of an octave can be used.

4. Two skips in a row should only be done using chord tones (arpeggios). Do not have a skip larger than a whole step unless it is from a chord to another chord tone. Do not skip more than a whole step from a chord tone.

5. Follow a skip by moving scalewise or chromatically in the opposite direction of the skip. A skip can also be followed with another skip in the opposite direction.

6. Change direction in motion at least once per measure.

7. Over a basic chord (i.e., G7), use the notes of that chord's embellishment (i.e., G7♭9) in the solo. For example, over a Dm7 you could play the notes from a Dm9. Over Cmaj7, you could outline a Cmaj9. Over an E7, you could play the notes from an E13♭9.

8. Use upper chord tones (7, 9, 11, and 13) in the solo and emphasize them by playing them on heavy beats. For example, over Am7, use the G (the seventh) and B (the ninth) notes. An example of this is shown below.

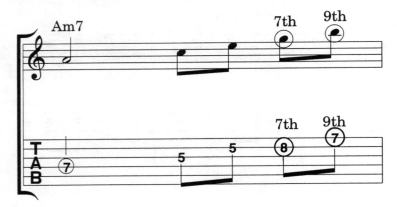

If you don't know the location of the upper chord tones, refer to the section in this book on "Chord Construction." The diagrams in that section show the location of the upper chord tones.

Notice the use of upper chord tones and the use of arpeggiating chord embellishments in the following example. The upper chord tones have been circled and labeled. The embellished chords which are being arpeggiated are written in parentheses above the original chords.

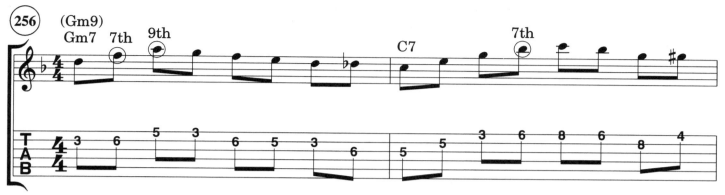

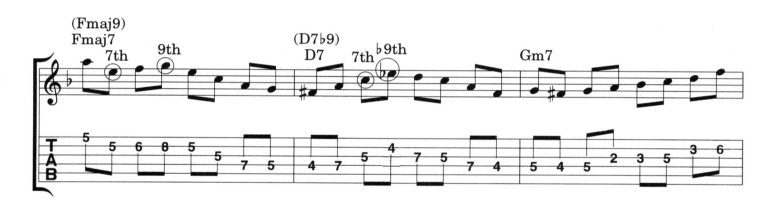

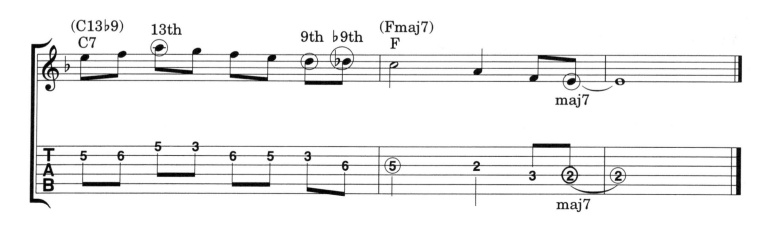

Secondary Arpeggios

The term *secondary arpeggio* refers to superimposing the arpeggio of one chord while another chord is being played. To *superimpose* an arpeggio means while one chord is being played in the accompaniment (rhythm), the arpeggio of another chord is being played by the soloist. For example, the accompanist could be playing Am7 and the soloist playing the notes in a Cmaj7 chord. Using certain secondary arpeggios can give your solos more of an "outside" sound. The term "playing outside" refers to playing single note lines or chords which are not in the key that is suggested by the music. An example of this would be playing an Eb7 arpeggio over a C7 chord.

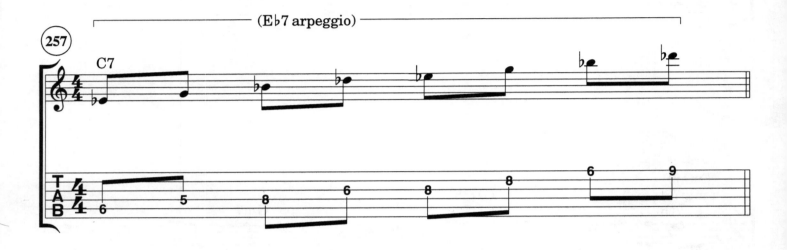

The secondary arpeggio being played will generally contain contain a note (or notes) which is in the original written chord. The secondary arpeggio will often sound better if it were to begin on that common note. In the following example, the Eb7 arpeggio is played over the C7 chord. The Eb7 arpeggio begins on the G note because G is the note which in contained in both the Eb7 and the C7 chords.

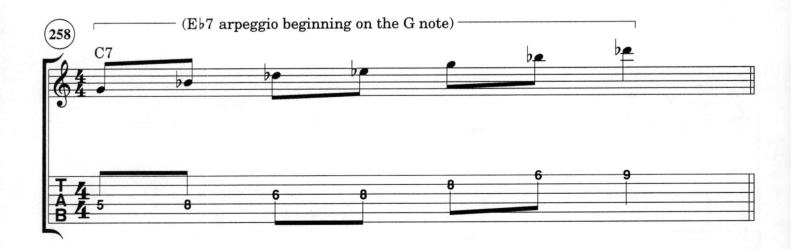

Secondary arpeggios work because by outlining a chord of a different name you are actually outlining an embellishment of the original chord. If I play a Dm7 arpeggio over a G7 chord, I am actually outlining a G11 chord. The notes in a G11 chord are: G, B, D, F, A, and C. The notes in a Dm7 chord are : D, F, A, and C. Notice that all of the notes in a Dm7 chord are contained in the G11 chord.

The following chart shows which secondary arpeggios can be played over various types of chords. The chords on the right can be arpeggiated while the chords on the left are played by the accompanist. The chart uses C and Am chords as examples. It is important to see the relationship of the C (or Am) chord to the arpeggiated chords and then be able to transpose and use the secondary arpeggios for any letter name chord.

Written in parentheses after the chords being arpeggiated are the scale relationships of the arpeggiated chords to the original chords.

Chord played by the rhythm	Chord being arpeggiated
C (maj7)	Am7 (vi)
C	Em7 (iii)
C	Gmaj7 (V)
Am7	Cmaj7 (III - minor scale)
Am7	Fmaj7 (VI)
Am7	Gmaj7 (♭VII)
Am7	Em7 (v)
Am7	D7 (IV)
C7	Gm7 (v)
C7	B♭maj7 (♭VII)
C7	Fm7(iv)
C7	D♭maj7(♭II)
C7	E♭maj7(♭III)
C7	G♭7 (♭V)

Secondary arpeggios can not only be used against the original chords shown on the left of the chart, but they can also be used with embellishments of the original chords. For example, B♭7 can be arpeggiated over a C7 chord, and B♭7 can also be arpeggiated over C9 and /or C13 chords.

The following examples contain secondary arpeggios. Written in parentheses above the measures are the names of the chords which are being arpeggiated.

secondary arpeggio for B♭maj7

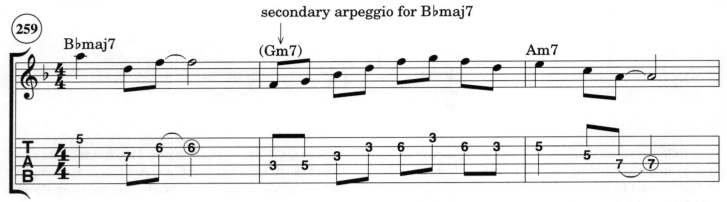

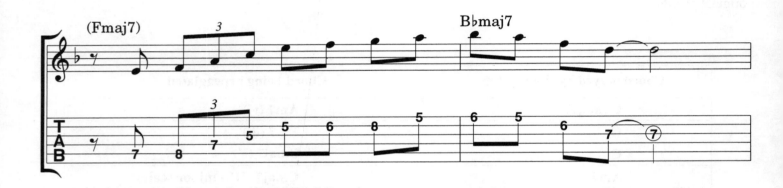

Be careful not to over-use secondary arpeggios. Written below is a progression with secondary arpeggio possibilities written in brackets above the original chords. Practice improvising solos to the original chord progression and occasionally throw in a secondary arpeggio.

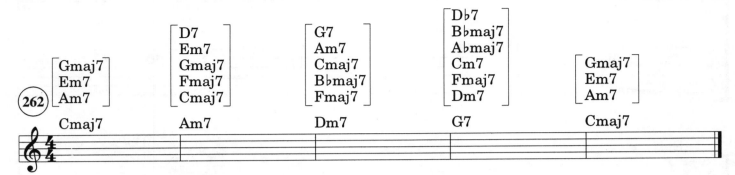

Because Dm7 is the ii chord in the key of C, all of the triads from the key of C can be played over Dm7. This same concept can be applied to any other minor chord. Treat the minor chord as the ii chord (even if it isn't) and outline triads from the key of its I chord. The next example and solo show how triads in the key of C are played over the Dm7 chord.

The Parker Cycle

Another way of achieving an outside sound would be to use the concept of the *Parker cycle*. The Parker cycle was often used by the great jazz saxophonist Charlie Parker. This technique is a type of secondary arpeggio, but it is unique enough that it will be presented in this section of the book.

The main idea behind the Parker cycle is to superimpose a 7th chord which is a minor third (three frets) above the 7th chord which is being played by the accompanist. For example, if the accompanist is playing a C7 chord, you play the notes in an E♭7 over it.

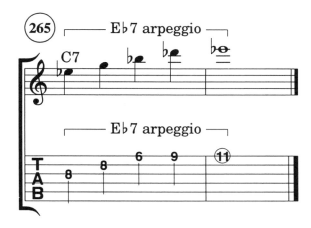

This works because the E♭7 chord contains the altered notes of a C7 chord.

The E♭ (D♯) in the E♭7 is the ♯9 of C7, and the D♭ in the E♭7 chord is the ♭9 of C7. The other two notes in the E♭7 chord (G and B♭) are already in the C7 chord. In essence, when you play an E♭7 arpeggio against a C7 chord, you are actually outlining a C7♯9♭9 chord.

The chart below shows the relationship of the notes in E♭7 to the notes in the C7 chord. Notice some of the same notes are contained in both chords. That's what makes the Parker cycle work.

C7 = C   E   G B♭
                ↑ ↑
E♭7 = E♭(D♯) G B♭ D♭
Relationship to C7 → ♯9   5 ♭7 ♭9

E♭7 is contained in C7♯9♭9
┌─────── C7♯9♭9 ───────┐
C E G B♭ D♯(E♭) D♭
        └─── E♭7 ───┘

Play the following example which uses the notes in an E♭7 chord over a C7.

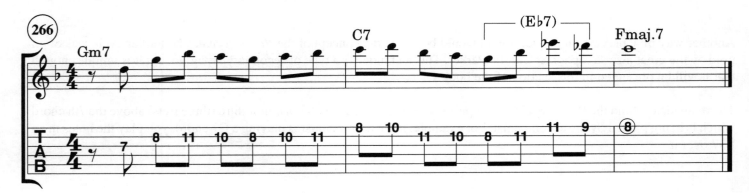

This concept can be taken another step further. Rather than using the notes in an E♭7 over a C7 chord, go up another minor third from the E♭7 (to G♭7) and use the notes of that chord over the C7 chord. So, you are now using the notes of the chord which is two minor thirds above the chord which the rhythm is playing.

The chart below shows the relationship of the notes in G♭7 to the notes in C7

$$C7 \; = C \;\; E \;\; G \;\; B♭$$

$$G♭7 = G♭ \;\; B♭ \;\; D♭ \;\; F♭♭(E)$$
Relationship to C7 → ♭5 ♭7 ♭9 3

G♭7 is contained in C7♭5♭9

C7♭5♭9
C E G♭ B♭ D♭
G♭7

Play the next example which uses the notes from G♭7 against the C7 chord.

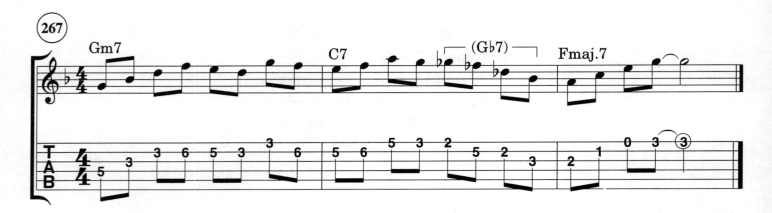

This process is repeated again going up another minor third. For example, using A7 against C7 (A7 is three sets of minor thirds above C7).

The following chart shows the relationship of the notes in A7 to the notes in C7.

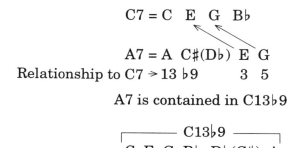

A7 is contained in C13♭9

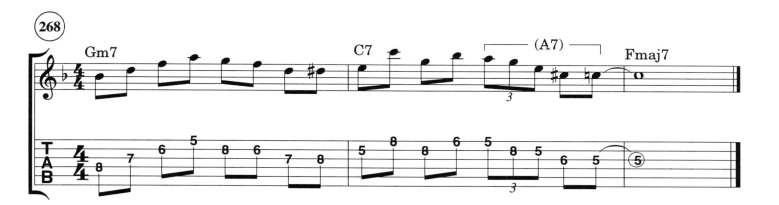

The next example shows how the notes of an A7 can be used over a C7 chord.

The diagram below shows how the Parker cycle is built. You can see that by going up in minor thirds four times you will then start over on the first chord (C).

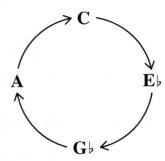

This concept of outlining chords a minor third higher will also work with minor chords and also seventh chords. For example, if a Dm7 chord is being played, you can outline an Fm7 chord. You could go up another minor third and outline an A♭m7, or you could go up yet another minor third an outline a Bm7 chord.

The charts below show the relationship of the notes in Fm7, A♭m7, and Bm7 to the notes in Dm7.

Dm7 =   D   F   A   C

Fm7 =   F   A♭   C   E♭
           ♭3   ♭5   ♭7   ♭9   ← Note relationship to Dm7

┌───── Dm7♭5♭9 ─────┐
D   F   A♭   C   E♭   ← Notes in Dm7♭5♭9
└───── Fm7 ─────┘   ← Notes in Fm7

───────────────────────────────

Dm7 =   D   F   A   C

A♭m7 =   A♭   C♭ (B) E♭   G♭
           ♭5   6   ♭9   ♭11   ← Note relationship to Dm7

┌───── Dm6♭5♭9♭11 ─────┐
D   F   A♭   B   E♭   G♭(F♯)
└───────── A♭m7 ─────────┘

───────────────────────────────

Dm7 =   D   F   A   C

Bm7 =   B   D   F♯ (G♭) A
           6   R   ♭11   5   ← Note relationship to Dm7

┌───── Dm6♭11 ─────┐
D   F   A   B   G♭(F♯)
└───── Bm7 ─────┘

Over Dm7 play the notes from Fm7 or A♭m7 or Bm7.

In the following example, the Parker cycle is used for a Dm7 chord. The rhythm section is playing a Dm7 chord but the solo uses the notes from an Fm7 chord.

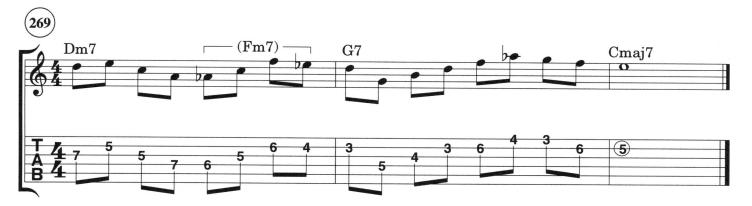

This can be very valuable in playing against chord progressions such as the ii-V-I progression. We discussed earlier in this book how common and important the ii-V-I progression is. Now, using Parker cycle, you can make your solo even more interesting.

Lets say you are improvising to the ii-V-I progression in the key of C.

Dm7– – – – – G7– – – – – – C

Rather than outlining the original chords or using the C major scale, try outline chords which are a minor third (or more than one minor third) above the original chords. For example, against Dm7 use Fm7, and against G7 use B♭7.

The chart below shows the various substituted chords which could be outlined.

For: Dm7– – – – G7 – – – – Cmaj7
Use: Fm7– – – – B♭7 – – – –Cmaj7
or: A♭m7– – – – D♭7– – – – Cmaj7
or: Bm7 – – – – E7 – – – – Cmaj7

Practice the following solo in which the Parker cycle is used to play over various ii-V-I progressions. The chords which are being outlined in the solo are written in parentheses above the chords which are played by the rhythm section.

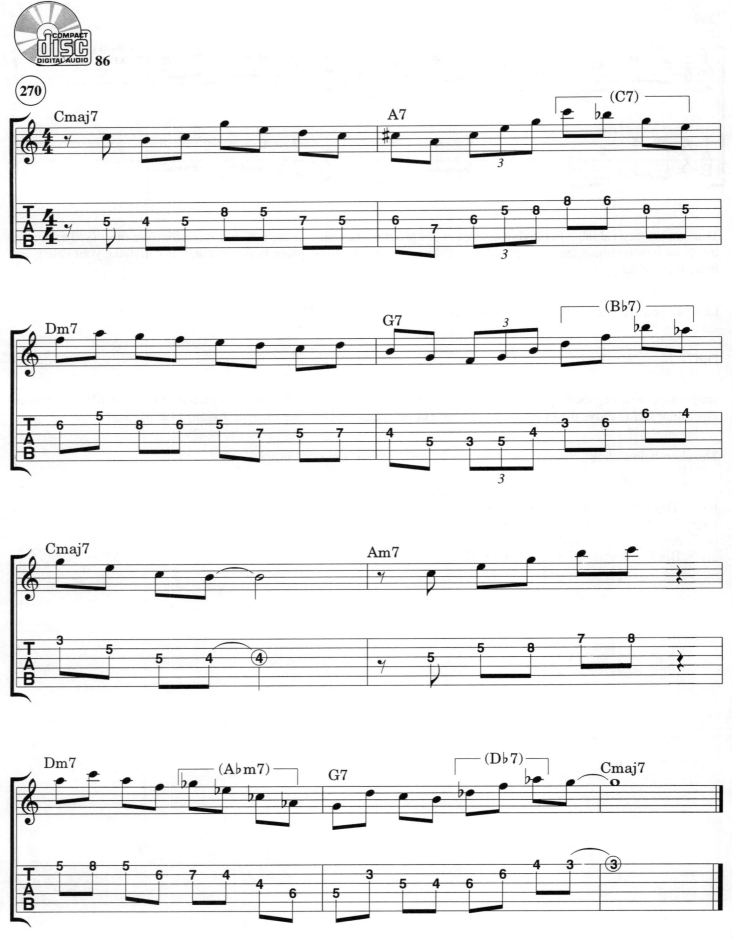

The Coltrane Cycle

The *Coltrane cycle* is named after another one of the great jazz horn players, John Coltrane, who frequently used this concept. The Coltrane cycle is similar to the Parker cycle in that the notes of one chord are played while a chord with a different name is played by the rhythm section.

The theory behind the Coltrane cycle is that against any chord you can superimpose a chord which is the same type and a major third or augmented fifth higher. For example, for a Dm7 chord you could use the notes from F#m7 (F#m7 is a major third above Dm7), or you could use the notes from A#m7. A#m7 (B♭m7) is an augmented fifth above Dm7. This concept can be very helpful in creating outside sounds to the ii-V-I progression. The chart below shows how the Coltrane cycle can be used with the ii-V-I progression.

For: Dm7 – – – – G7 – – – – Cmaj7

Use: F#m7 – – – B7 – – – – Cmaj7

Or: A#m7(B♭m7)-D#7(E♭7) – – – Cmaj7

Practice the following examples using the Coltrane cycle. The superimposed chords from which the notes are taken for the portions of the solo are written in parentheses above the original chords to be played by the accompanist.

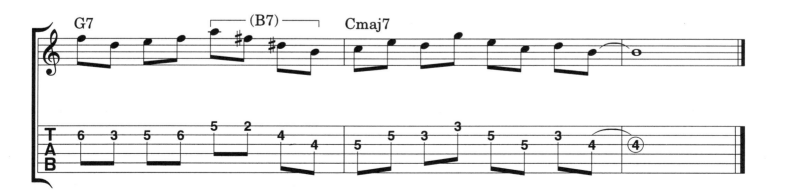

227

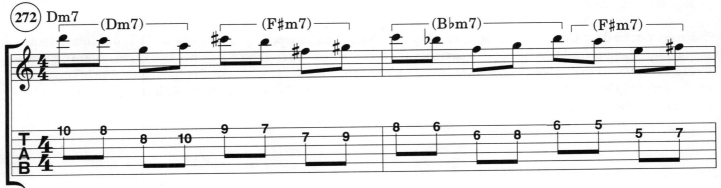

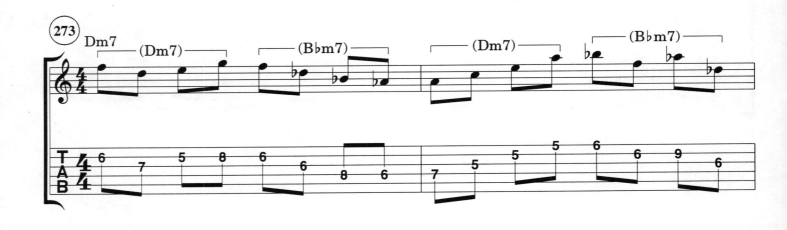

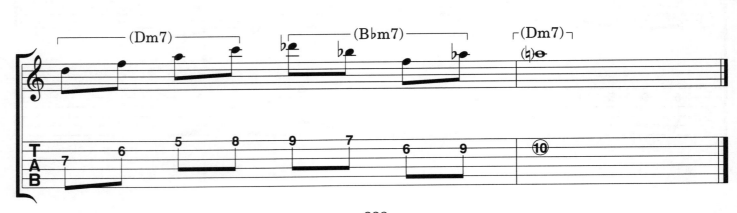

Improvising Around A Melody

To be able to improvise around a given melody is one of the most sophisticated techniques used in improvisation. It requires the player to "control" the improvisation and really think about what notes are being played rather than "free-falling" and being able to use anything at anytime. There are several techniques which can be used to help you develop this skill. A good first step in improvising around the original melody would be to alter some of the rhythms of the original melody. For example, two quarter notes in a row could be changed to two eighth notes followed by a pause for one beat. Also, the first note in a measure could be anticipated and played on the "and" of beat four in the previous measure. Long notes could be anticipated and played 1/2 beat earlier. Another possibility is to turn two quarter notes in a row into a dotted quarter followed by an eighth note.

The next examples show how the rhythms in *She'll Be Comin' 'Round The Mountain* could be altered. The first example is the basic original melody, and the second example shows the same melody with the rhythms altered.

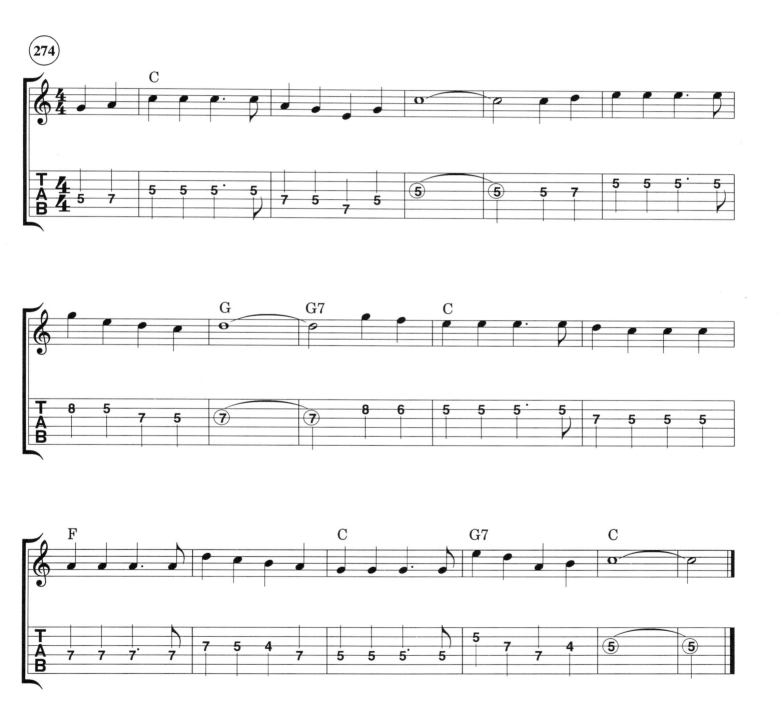

229

Another technique in improvising around a given melody is to improvise in the "holes" in the melody. These "holes" are places where the melody pauses. They can be ties, long notes, or rests. Written below is the melody to *She'll Be Comin' 'Round The Mountain*. The circled areas show where the holes are. These will be the spots where you will improvise.

The notes you use for the improvisation can come from any of the concepts you have learned (i.e. arpeggios, scales, tonal centers, secondary arpeggios, modes, Parker cycle, Coltrane cycle, etc.). In the following example, some improvisation has been written where the holes occurred in the melody. Notice how the improvised sections blend in well with the melody. The improvised portions begin and end with notes close to the original melody notes. Practice this written solo and then practice playing your own improvisations in the holes. As with all of your other first attempts at improvisation, you should write out your solos.

In the next example, the melody is embellished even more by improvising not only in the long gaps, but also where dotted notes and ties occurred. Also, in the next example, chord substitution and embellishment have been used. Using the notes from the embellished and substituted chords is an effective tool in the improvisation.

After you have practiced improvising in the holes, the next step is to leave out some of the melody. You should still improvise in the holes, but now leave out entire sections of the melody. The portions of the melody to leave out should be phrases (from one pause to another). Try not to omit too much of the melody.

In the next example, *She'll Be Comin' 'Round The Mountain* has been written out again, and the circled areas show where portions of the melody have been left out and an improvisation has been written in. Improvisation also occurs in the "holes" in the melody. Play the written solo and then create your own versions. Notice the use of the F#dim as a passing chord connecting F to C/G (C with G in the bass).

234

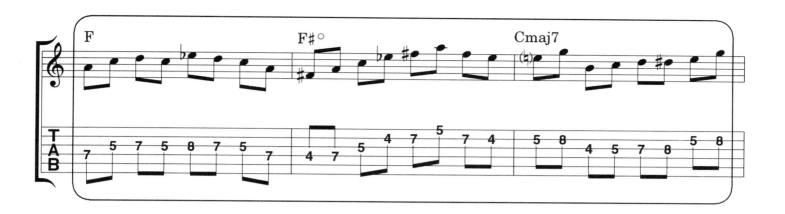

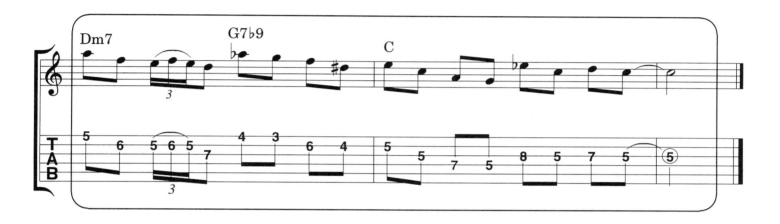

The same technique you are using to improvise to *She'll Be Comin' 'Round The Mountain* can be use on any jazz standard. Practice improvising in the melodic holes and also leaving out portions of the melody. Each time the piece is repeated, more and more of the melody can be left out until total improvisation is used. On the last time through, the original (unedited) melody is played again. This is a common format in jazz.

Another very effective tool in learning to improvise around a melody is to use the same rhythms as the original melody, only play different notes.

In the first example below, the melody to *Silent Night* is written. In the second example, the same rhythms have been used as in the original melody, but the notes are different. Practice this solo and then write out a new melody using the same rhythms from the original *Silent Night*. Notice the use of chord embellishment and chord substitution to enhance the new melody.

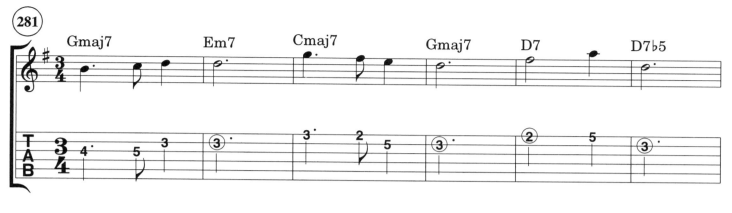

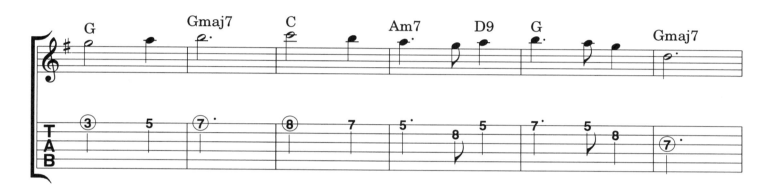

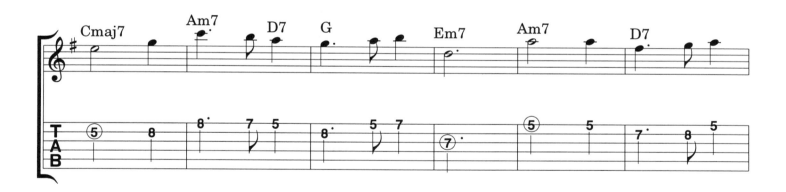

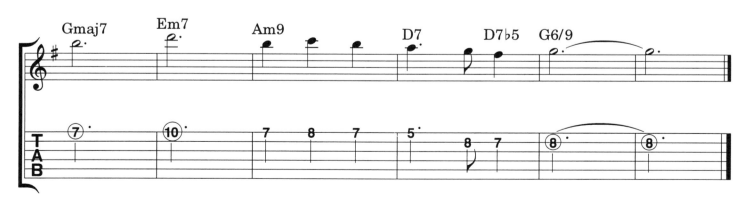

After creating a new melody, you could improvise in the holes and around the new melody using the concepts presented earlier in this section of the book.

Here are some rules to follow when improvising around a melody. These same rules are valuable considerations to be made for any kind of improvisation.

1. **Use scales, modes, arpeggios, secondary arpeggios, etc.**
2. **Try to make the heavy (important) beats be chord tones. Generally, this will happen on the first beat of each measure, or beats one and three in 4/4 and beat one in 3/4.**
3. **Avoid a series of large skips. If you make them, make the notes chord tones.**
4. **Follow a skip by moving scalewise in the opposite direction.**
5. **Try to change the direction of the line at least one time in a measure.**

Quartal Harmony

One of the most distinguishing characteristics of modern jazz and fusion (combining styles of jazz and rock) guitar playing is the use of *quartal harmony* and intervals of fourths. With quartal harmony, chords are built by notes being stacked in fourths rather than in thirds. The chords we have used so far in this book have been built in thirds. Building chords in thirds is called *terciary harmony*. For example, the minor triad is built with a root, then a note which is a minor third above the root, and finally another note which is a major third above that note. In quartal harmony, the notes of the chord are a fourth apart. For example, Dm7sus contains D, G, C, and F. The notes of the Dm7sus chord are separated by the interval of a fourth. The use of this type of harmony will give your solos a very contemporary sound.

There are two types of chords which are built on fourths: the m7sus chord, and the 6/9 chord. Both of these types of chords are built in fourths. For example, the notes in a Cm7sus chord are: C, F, Bb, and Eb. Drawn below are two fingerings of the m7sus chord. The one on the left has the root on the fifth string, and the one on the right has the root on the fourth string. The chart above the diagrams shows the fret location of the roots on strings five and four.

Location Of Roots

5th String

Fret ———➤	0	2	3	5	7	8	10	12
Root Name ➤	A	B	C	D	E	F	G	A

4th String

Fret ———➤	0	2	3	5	7	9	10	12
Root Name ➤	D	E	F	G	A	B	C	D

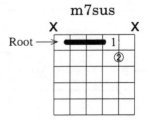

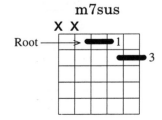

Like barre chords, the m7sus chord patterns can be moved around the neck. Wherever the chord is positioned, the name of the note which is the root (on the fifth or fourth strings) will be the letter name of the chord.

Practice playing the following chord progression which uses m7sus chords.

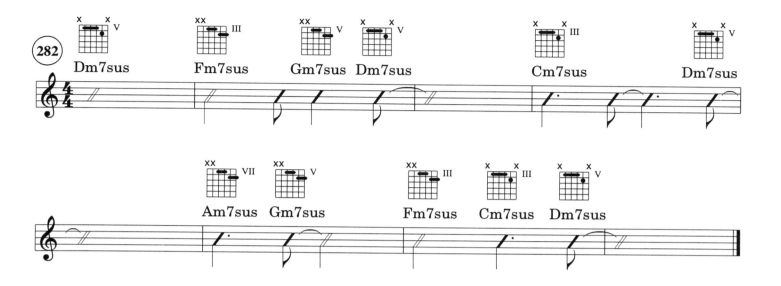

Another type of chord which is built in fourths is the major 6/9 chord. The fingering pattern for this chord is drawn below.

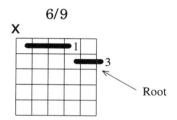

Notice this fingering for the 6/9 chord has the root of the chord on the first string, and the third of the chord on the lowest string played. It is voiced this way so the notes of the chord are a fourth apart (quartal harmony). For example, the G6/9 chord consists of G, B, D, E, and A notes. It would be fingered with the G note on the first string, and the B note (the third) on the fifth string. With the notes of the chord aligned in this way, the notes in the chord (from low to high) are: B, E, A, D, and G. The notes in the chord are now separated by the interval of a fourth.

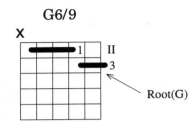

G6/9

This chord pattern can also be moved around the neck. Wherever the chord is positioned, the name of the root note (on the first string) will be the letter name of the chord.

Location Of Roots

1st String

Fret ⟶	0	1	3	5	7	8	10	12
Root Name ⟶	E	F	G	A	B	C	D	E

Practice the following chord progressions using 6/9 chords.

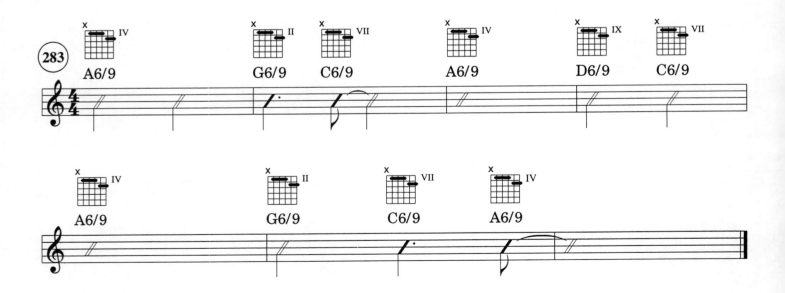

Playing The Blues Using Quartal Harmony

The m7sus and 6/9 chords can be used to play accompaniment and/or solos. In the blues, these chords can be used to create a *chord solo*. To play a blues chord solo using the m7sus chord, the m7sus chords to be used are those in which the highest note in the chord is a note from the blues scale of the key in which you are playing. For example, if you are playing the blues in the key of C, the notes in the C blues scale are: C, E♭, F, G♭, G, and B♭. To play a blues chord solo in the key of C using the m7sus chord form, use the m7sus chords which are positioned so the highest note in the chord (first or second string) is one of the notes from the C blues scale. The patterns below show m7sus chords that could be used for blues in the key of C.

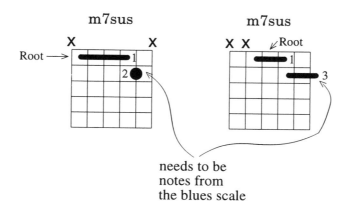

needs to be notes from the blues scale

Chords Which Can Be Used For Blues In C

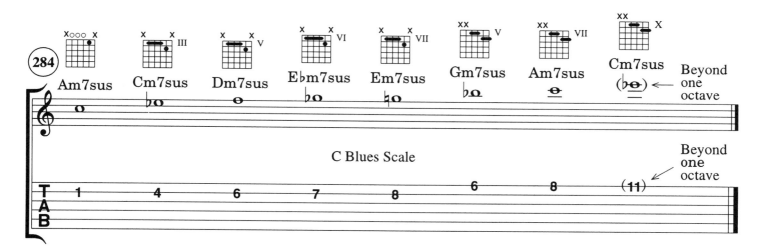

The following blues solo shows how m7sus chords can be used in the key of C. The chords which would be played for the accompaniment to the solo are written boldly in squares above the measures. Notice each of the m7sus which harmonize the blues scale in the key can be used at any time in the solo regardless of what the accompaniment chords are. The notes written on the staff show what the highest note of the m7sus chord should be. This will help you to determine where to position the m7sus chord. Don't play the single notes, but play the m7sus chord with the written notes on the top. The original chords to the progression are written in squares above the measures.

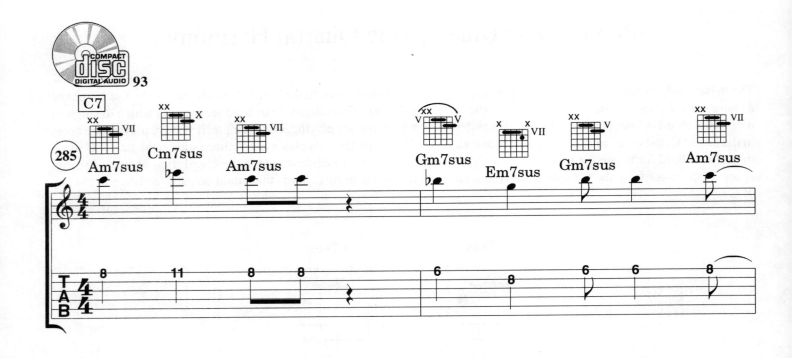

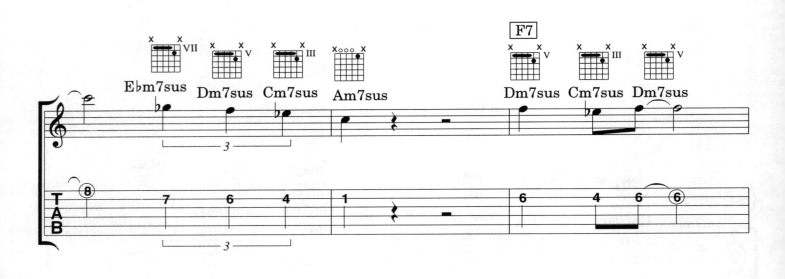

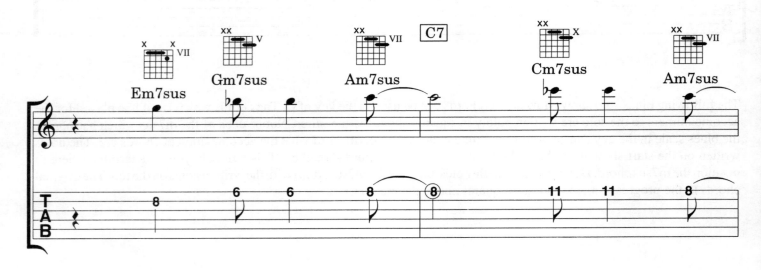

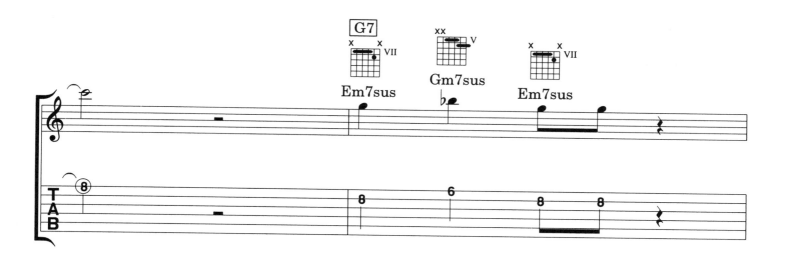

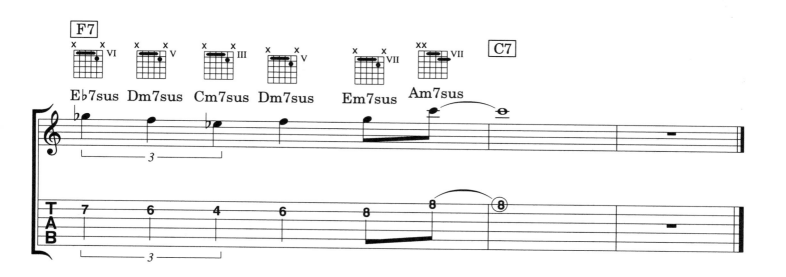

6/9 chords can also be used to create a blues chord solo. When using the 6/9 chord forms, the note on the **first string** of the chord pattern should be a note from the blues scale of the key in which you are playing. For example, the notes in the G blues scale are: G, B♭, C, D♭, D, and F. If you are playing a blues chord solo in the key of G, the 6/9 chords which could be used should have one of these notes on the first string.

The following diagrams show which 6/9 chords could be used to solo in the key of G.

Chords Which Can Be Used For Blues In G

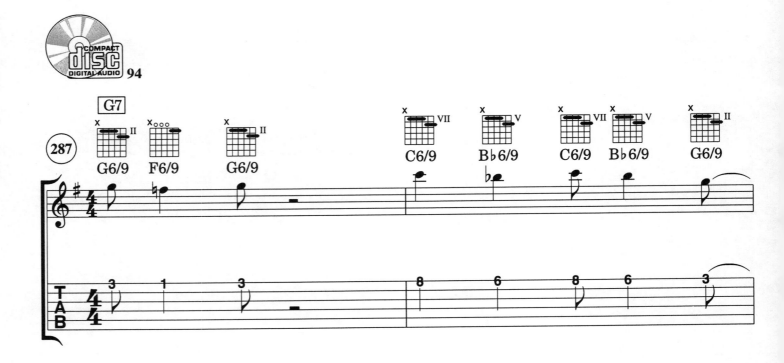

Play the following solo which is a blues chord solo in the key of G using 6/9 chords. Notice again that any of the 6/9 chords which harmonize the G blues scale can be used at any time in the solo regardless of which of the three chords in the blues progression is being played in the accompaniment. Again, the original chords to the progression are written in squares above the measures.

244

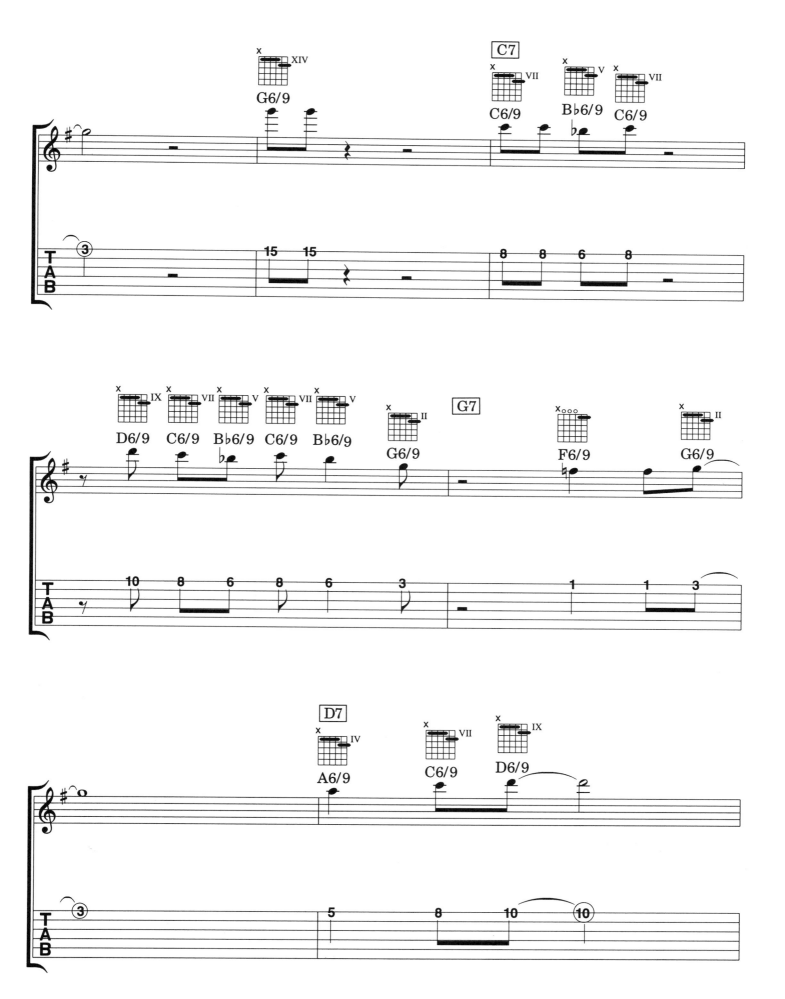

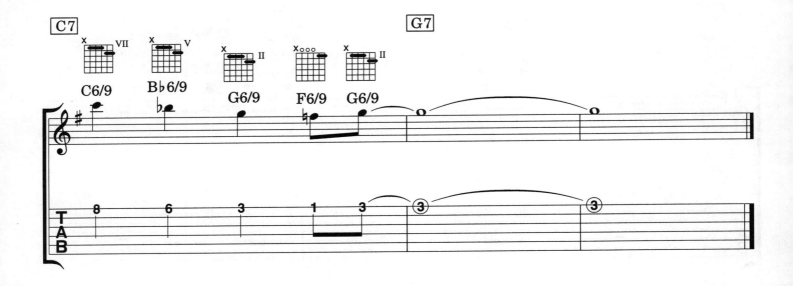

Chord Substitution Using Quartal Harmony

The m7sus and 6/9 chords can also be used to substitute for other chords. On the chart below, the chords on the left show the original chords, and on the right are listed the various m7sus chords which can be substituted in place of the original chords.

Cm9, Cm7	Cm7sus, Dm7sus, Gm7sus, Am7sus
C9	Dm7sus, Em7sus, Gm7sus, Am7sus

As you can see, for a m9 or m7 chord m7sus chords can be substituted which are the same letter name, up a whole step, up a fifth, or up a sixth. For the ninth chord, the substituted chords are m7sus chords which are a whole step higher, a major third higher, a fifth higher, or a sixth higher. This type of substitution works because the notes of the substituted chords are notes which would embellish the original chord. For example, a Gm7sus chord will substitute for a Cm9 chord. The notes in a Gm7sus chord are G, B♭, D, F, and C. The G is the fifth of Cm9, B♭ is the flat seventh of Cm9, D is the ninth of Cm9, F is the eleventh of Cm9, and C is the root of Cm9. By playing Gm7sus against Cm9, in a sense you are playing Cm11.

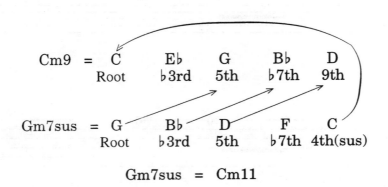

246

The following chord progressions have the original chords written on the top and the m7sus substituted chords written on the bottom. For the m7sus chords, use the chord forms (fifth or fourth string roots) which will make the chord changes convenient and keep them close together.

95

(288)

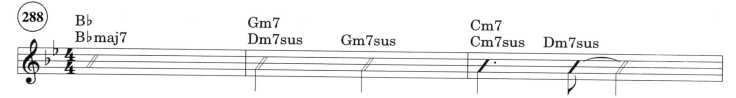

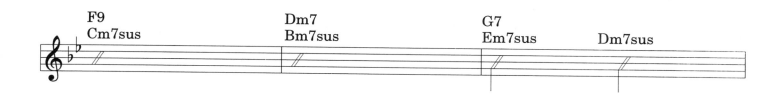

(289)

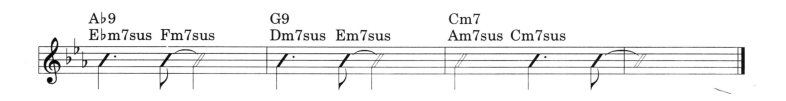

247

6/9 chords can also be used as substitution chords. On the following chart, the original chords are written on the left and the 6/9 chords which can be substituted in their place are written on the right. Remember, the root of the 6/9 chord is on the first string.

Cm9, Cm7	B♭6/9, E♭6/9, F6/9
C9	B♭6/9, C6/9, F6/9

For a m7 or m9 chord, 6/9 chords can be substituted if they are down a whole step, up a minor third, or up a fourth. For ninth chords, 6/9 chords can be substituted if they are down a whole step, have the same letter name, or up a fourth.

The following progressions have the original chords written on the top and the substituted 6/9 chords written on the bottom.

248

Single Note Soloing Using Fourths

Another common technique used in fusion style playing is using the interval of a fourth in the single line solo. A series of fourths in a solo give the solo line a very contemporary sound. In playing a single note solo using fourths, the notes which are used often come from the chord (or a substituted chord) which is built on fourths (m7sus, or 6/9 chords). The following examples show some short melodic ideas or "licks" which use the interval of a fourth. Notice the chord with which each lick is played.

The following solo contains sections where the interval of a fourth is used. So they can be easily seen, the fourths have been circled.

Often, the notes in the solo which move in fourths are derived from m7sus and 6/9 chord substitutions. The following solo illustrates how this could be done. The entire solo is over a Dm7 chord. Written in parentheses are the substituted chords which contain the fourths used in the solo.

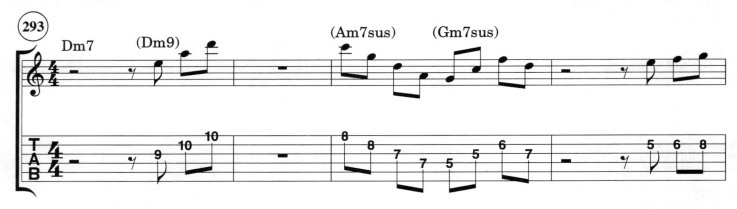

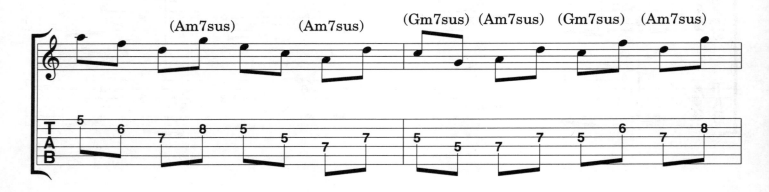

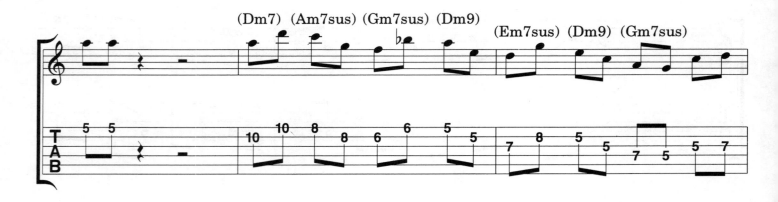

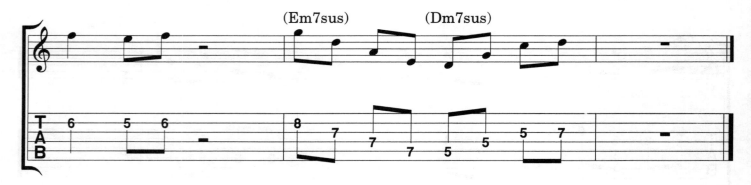

Geometrical Shapes

Geometrical shapes are created by forming a fingering pattern, and then moving that form (pattern) to a different set of strings and/or frets. For example, the following shows a geometrical shape. Written under the diagram are the notes in the shape. The line connecting the dots shows how the shape is formed.

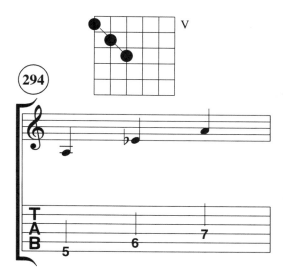

Although the diagrams in this section are written with a fret number next to them, they are moveable and can begin in any fret. Also, the diagrams in this section of the book show the geometrical shapes beginning on the sixth string; however, the shapes may begin and end on any string.

The same pattern as in the previous example can be moved to an adjacent string, as shown below.

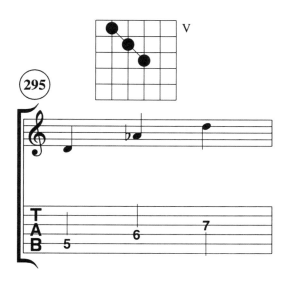

The pattern could also be moved up (or down) one fret.

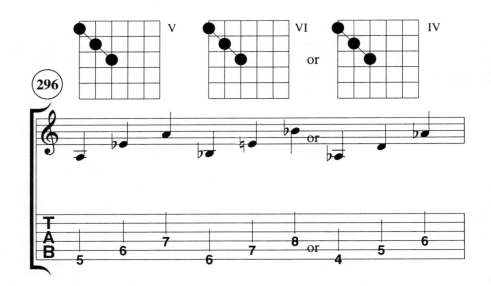

The patterns (geometrical shapes) can be repeated moving straight across the string, or up or down frets. The rule is: **don't skip a fret or a string.** Play notes on the same string or adjacent strings and in consecutive frets.

The following shows a geometrical shape which is moved across the strings. The notes which are played are written under the diagram.

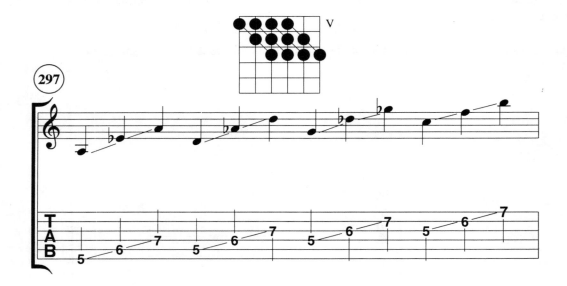

Here are some other examples of geometrical shapes which move across the strings.

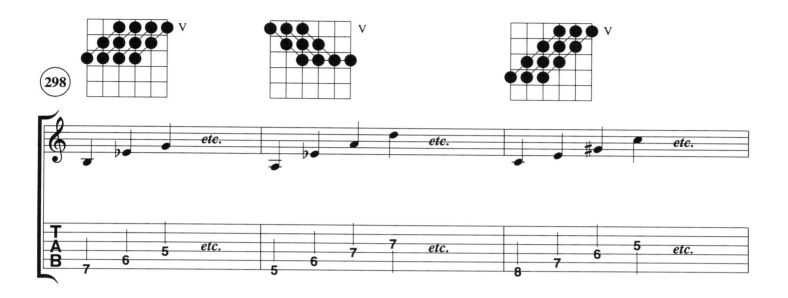

The following diagram shows a geometrical shape which is continually moving down one fret.

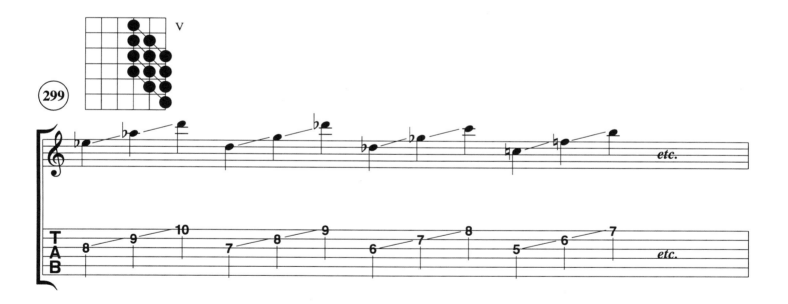

Geometrical shapes sound best when used with chords from the dominant seventh family. However, they can be used with any chord depending on how "outside" you want the sound to be. They will generally sound best if they are used only briefly, and if the pattern begins on a chord tone from the chord being played by the accompanist. The theory behind the use of geometrical shapes is that the "togetherness," or unique sound of the shape outweighs the fact that some of the notes are dissonant with the chord.

The following solo contains geometrical shapes. The sections where the shapes have been used are circled.

Practice creating and using your own geometrical shapes.

Table Of Scales And Their Uses

Scale Type	Chord For Which The Scale Can Be Used
Major (Ionian Mode)	major, maj7, maj9, 6, add 9, sus, any basic chord in the major key
Natural Minor	minor, m7, m6, m9, m7sus
Harmonic Minor	minor, m7, m6, m9, m+7, m7sus
Melodic Minor	minor, m7, m6, m9, m+7, m7sus
Jazz Minor	minor, m7, m6, m9, m+7, m7sus
Dorian Mode	minor, m7, m9, m7sus
Phrygian Mode	minor, m7, m9, m7sus, major chords (for a flamenco quality)
Lydian Mode	major, maj7, maj9, maj7♯11 (maj7♭5)
Mixolydian Mode	7, 9, 11, 13, altered sevenths
Aeolian Mode	minor, m7, m6, m9
Locrian Mode	dim, m7♭5
Super Locrian Mode	dominant seventh chord 1/2 step lower
Diminished (Whole-Half)	dim
Diminished (Half-Whole)	7♭9, 7♯9
Whole Tone	aug, +7, 7+, 7♯5, 7♭5
Blues Scale	7, 9, 11, 13, 7♯9, minor, m7, m9

Great Music at Your Fingertips